D1301187

Math Mind Games

Heinrich Hemme

Illustrations by Matthias Schwoerer

FEB 3 '03

j QA95.H46 2002
Hemme, Heinrich.
Math mind games
New York : Sterling Pub.,
c2002.

Sterling Publishing Co., Inc.
New York

Library of Congress Cataloging-in-Publication Data available

10 9 8 7 6 5 4 3 2 1

Published by Sterling Publishing Company, Inc.
387 Park Avenue South, New York, N.Y. 10016
Excerpted from the title *Mathematischer Denkspass,* originally published by
Weltbild Verlag GmbH, Augsburg, Germany
© 1998 by Weltbild Verlag GmbH, Augsburg, Germany
English translation © 2002 by Sterling Publishing Co., Inc.
Distributed in Canada by Sterling Publishing
c/o Canadian Manda Group, One Atlantic Avenue, Suite 105
Toronto, Ontario, Canada M6K 3E7
Distributed in Australia by Capricorn Link (Australia) Pty. Ltd.
P.O. Box 704, Windsor, NSW 2756 Australia

Manufactured in China
All rights reserved

Sterling ISBN 0-8069-7691-8

CONTENTS

PREFACE

In his book *The Canterbury Puzzles*, which was published in 1907, the great English puzzle-inventor H.E. Dudeney wrote that it was possible to make puzzles out of almost anything—coins, matches, game tiles, wires, strings, letters, and numbers.

Dudeney did not exaggerate: Even in normal everyday life, questions arise again and again that are alluring for people who love to rack their brains. That's what the forty-plus puzzles in this book are about—common everyday questions that can come up in the life of any one of us at any time.

Since we ourselves are not mathematicians, we are not posing any questions that can be answered only by mathematicians. On the contrary, the logic problems, and even a number of the geometrical tasks, do not require any knowledge of mathematics and can be solved just by using common sense. For most of the others, you probably won't need much more than junior high school math.

Most of the puzzles were first published as "Prize Puzzles for Thinkers" in the column "Cogito" from 1990 to 1997. We wish you a lot of fun solving them!

Heinrich Hemme

The Mind Games

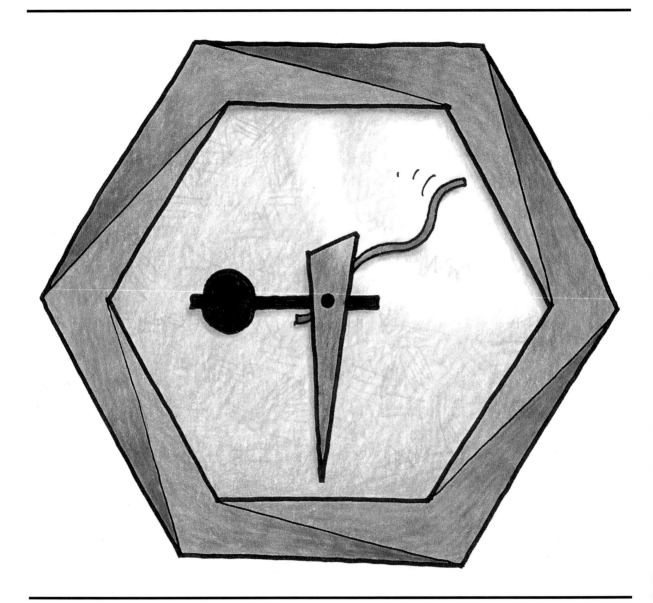

1. THE HEXAGONAL CLOCK

For her birthday, my wife wanted a clock for the mantle above the fireplace. It could not be just any mantle clock, but a particular one she had shown me in the window of a shop we walked by during a Sunday stroll. So I let her have her wish and gave her the clock.

This clock was not ordinary, but the product of a modern designer. The case, made of fine-grained, reddish beechwood, had a matte lacquer finish and was shaped like a hexagonal box, standing on one of its sides. The hexagonal face was not actually a clock-face at all—not a single number was written on it. Spots were not even marked where the numbers normally would be. You had to guess the time from the positions of the clock's hands. I don't like this kind of affectation. I expect that a good clock will have the numbers 1 to 12 on it!

A couple of days after my wife's birthday, when I was alone in the living room for a minute, I couldn't resist the temptation to take the clock and place it on a different side. The hands were in the wrong position, but other than that you couldn't see what I had done. When my wife returned to the room, I said casually, "I don't think your new clock is running correctly."

She glanced at it, smiled a bit smugly, and said, "Dear, you can't fool me with such simple-minded jokes." She got up, went to the fireplace, and put the clock back onto its correct side.

I was surprised. "How did you know right away that the clock was on its side?"

"When a clock tells the wrong time, the hands are still positioned in a way that makes sense. I mean, even though the time the clock shows may not be correct at the moment, it will be correct at some point. But when you place the clock on its side, it doesn't show any time correctly. For example, both hands point upward at noon, but when you place the clock upside down, both hands will point exactly downward. This position of the hands can never happen on a clock."

I thought about the clock the entire evening. While I was watching the late night news, an interesting question came to me: "How many sides must a clock have in order for the hour hand and the minute hand to make sense no matter which side the clock were placed on?"

I asked my wife. She didn't know.

Do you?

Answer on page 100.

2. THE OLD GRAVEL PIT

As a child, I liked to play behind my parents' house in an old gravel pit that had been closed down. Playing there was strictly forbidden, but who cared? In the course of the years, rainwater had gathered in the pit, and a pretty little pond had been created, which was perfect for swimming. All around the gravel pit were pine trees, birch trees, and junipers and some small sand hills. It was an ideal playground for the kids in the neighborhood, and I spent countless afternoons there, often coming home at dusk with torn and dirty pants and sweaters.

Many years later, when visiting my hometown, I went to our old gravel pit on a Sunday afternoon. How it had changed—I hardly recognized it! The city had bought the land and turned it into a small park. The landscape architect must have been a lover of geometrical shapes, because he had turned the gravel pit into a square pond, situated in the center of a square park. All around the pond were small patches of lawn, flower beds, and groups of trees. A path cut through them, circling the pond and touching the four sides of the park limits at their central points.

It seemed to me that the pond was much bigger than it had been when it was a gravel pit, but I'm not good at estimating such things. I only knew that the entire park, including the pond, covered an area of four acres.

Can you figure out how big the pond was?

Answer on page 100.

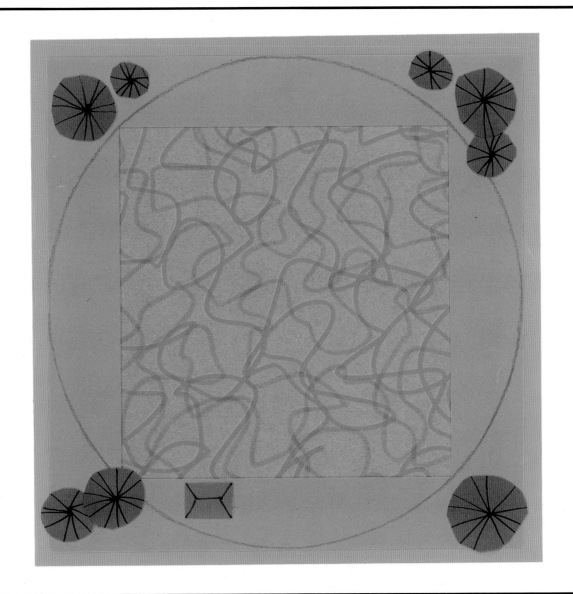

3. THE CHESSBOARD

My son Matthew got a child's tool chest for his eighth birthday from my brother-in-law, Ken. He had wanted it very badly, and the entire family was delighted at how happy he was with it. I was the only one who didn't have a good feeling about this present and, as we would soon find out, I was right.

That afternoon my son disappeared into the basement with his new tool chest and shortly after that, I heard quiet sawing noises from downstairs. First, I didn't think anything of it, but when the noises stopped and my son did not come back upstairs, I became suspicious. I knew Matthew. When he was quiet for a long period of time, he was either doing some mischief, or he had a bad conscience.

I went into the basement. Beaming with joy, he came running to me. "Look, Daddy, what I have sawed up!" He presented me with a pile of little wooden boards, all square and of the same size. I recognized them at once. "It's your old chessboard," he said. "I did it with my new fox-tail saw."

I became very angry. My beautiful old chessboard, a magnificent inlaid piece made of ebony and ivory, which I had inherited from my grandfather, had been sawn into its 64 squares!

"Daddy, guess how many saw-cuts I had to make!"

Of course, I did not guess, but gave Matthew a good piece of my mind and grounded him for the afternoon. But maybe you will do what my son asked me to do. How many straight cuts did he have to make, at the very least, in order to saw the chessboard into its 64 squares?

Note: You can assume that my son placed the pieces of the board that were already cut on top of each other and sawed through all of them at once.

Answer on page 101.

4. THE MATHBOARD

During her last year in kindergarten, my daughter Christina wanted nothing more than to be allowed to go to school. But then, when she had to go every day, she didn't enjoy it at all. Getting up early every morning was torture; she thought reading was boring, and writing was dumb. She preferred to draw what she wanted and not what her teacher wanted, and when she was supposed to do her homework, she would always end up in a fight with my wife. But the worst thing for Christina was math. Adding and subtracting was a misery for her, and she tried it only with the greatest reluctance.

That changed when my sister-in-law gave her a mathboard as a present. The mathboard had 60 square fields, and it came with a box of tiles, on which the numbers 1 to 100 were printed. Now, Christina could play with numbers, and she visibly lost her fear.

One evening, as Christina was coming upstairs to see me, I heard something fall and clatter down the stairs. It sounded like a handful of peas. A moment later, Christina came crying into my office.

"Daddy, I tripped on the stairs and all but three of the numbers fell off my board!" She sobbed and showed me her mathboard. The three tiles with the numbers 14, 29, and 46 were still on it.

I tried consoling her, and when she had calmed down a little, I asked, "How were the tiles arranged on your board?"

"I put down all the tiles from 1 to 60, and I was able to trace a path from 1 to 60 in order, moving only up, down, left, and right." Christina started to cry again. "And now, they all but three tiles fell off."

I took her in my arms and said, "Come on, we'll pick up the other tiles and then arrange them just like they were before."

It turned out to be a little trickier than I expected, but after half an hour we succeeded, and my daughter was laughing again.

Do you know which number had to be in the field in the lower right-hand corner?

Answer on page 101.

5. THE TABLE

"Oh, no! Aunt Clara wants to visit?" Aunt Clara is my wife's oldest sister, feared throughout the family for her nasty tongue and her nagging.

"She'll only be staying a week," my wife said, but she didn't look happy herself.

Suddenly, I remembered. "What on earth are we going to do about the table?"

During her last visit, five years ago, Aunt Clara had given us a table as a gift. It was a monstrosity made of massive, dark-stained oak with a round top and its legs were decorated with gewgaws. The table ruined the look of our beautiful, bright, living room, furnished in light-colored wood, and as soon as Aunt Clara left, we banished it to the basement. There it served as a workbench, and of course its top had suffered from the hammering, drilling, and sawing that took place on it.

We went into the basement and had a closer look at the table. "The legs are okay, but we'll have to have a new top made," my wife said.

I agreed. "I'll unscrew the top right away, and take it to the cabinetmaker tomorrow."

When I got home from work the next day, I couldn't find the tabletop anywhere. "Do you know where the tabletop is?" I asked my wife.

"The bulk garbage was being collected today so I had them take it away," she said.

"How could you?" I was horrified. "I haven't measured it yet, and if the new top is only one inch larger or smaller, Aunt Clara will see it at once. If I know her, she wrote down all the measurements of the table before giving it to us."

My wife tried to calm me down. "Don't get so upset. Clara would never know if the tabletop was a little larger or smaller, and besides, I know how we can figure out the size of the top."

She took me down into the basement. "You had pushed the table exactly into the corner, so that the top touched the walls and the corner of the cable-shaft." I nodded. "Now, we simply need the measurements of the cable-shaft," my wife continued.

I went to get a tape measure. The cable-shaft, which started at the ceiling and reached to the floor, stuck out 7 inches in one direction, and 14 inches in the other. The shaft formed right angles with the walls. My wife took a piece of paper and began to calculate. Then she gave the paper to me and said: "This is how big the tabletop was."

Do you know the diameter of the tabletop?

Answer on page 102.

6. THE LOLLIPOPS

It was a warm Sunday afternoon, and Uncle Al had come for a visit. The entire family was in the back yard, drinking lemonade and enjoying the gorgeous weather. Everyone was spellbound as Uncle Al told about the Alaskan cruise he had just taken. My son Matthew was not at all interested. Restlessly, he roamed about, hiding something behind his back. Finally, Uncle Al finished his story and leaned back comfortably. Matthew had been waiting for this moment. He brought his piggy bank from behind his back, placed it on the table in front of his uncle and looked at him expectantly, without saying anything.

"Well, let's see if I have something left for you," said Uncle Al. He stuck his hand into his pocket and came up with a bunch of coins that he dumped on the table. "These two are for your piggy bank." He put two coins in the slot. "And you can buy candy with the rest."

"Thanks a lot, Uncle Al!" Matthew said, beaming with delight. He counted the coins carefully—$2.16. He put the coins in his pants pocket and ran to the candy store down the street, where he spent it all on lollipops. On his way home, he passed the grocery store. The same lollipops that he had bought were in the window— on sale for one penny less than in the candy store! Matthew was terribly upset. In this store, he would have been able to get three more lollipops for the same amount of money.

Do you know how many lollipops Matthew had bought?

Answer on page 103.

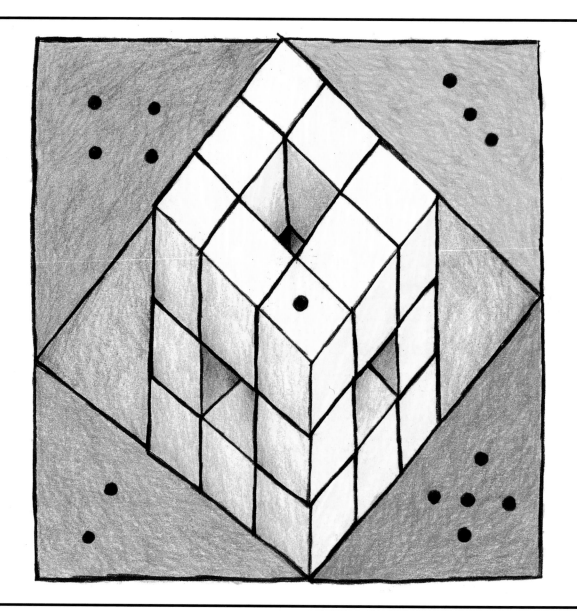

7. THE DIE

As every parent has experienced, the time of endless questions begins when a child is about 3 ½ years old. "Why does Swiss cheese have holes?" or "Why are bananas bent?" Unanswerable questions usually bring about new and even more difficult questions. Peace and quiet comes only in the evening when the child is safely tucked in bed and—hopefully—asleep. Generally, this stage passes in six months. Then parents can breathe easier—at least for a while!

However, my daughter seems to be the exception. In her case, this stage has yet to be completed. She is now 13 years old and continues to challenge me with questions to which I seldom have an answer.

The other day she came into my study with a bunch of dice glued together. There were 20 ordinary dice in the shape, and they formed a 3 × 3 × 3 cube with gaps along all three central axes, like the one in the illustration.

"Daddy, tell me how many dots are on the 72 surfaces that I did not cover when I glued the dice together."

Somewhat annoyed, I remarked that the dice she glued together came from a new set of games that I had just purchased. But I swallowed my anger and started to count. It was relatively easy to count the dots on the 48 surfaces that were on the faces of the large cube. Counting those that were in the hollow area gave me some trouble. Whenever I turned the large die, I forgot which dots I had already counted. After a few tries I gave up.

With a triumphant tone in her voice, my daughter said: "Please, Daddy, try again. I'll give you a hint. I only glued together surfaces that had the same number of dots. Now—that should make answering my question a breeze!"

Well, I respectfully disagreed, because I could make no sense out of the hint.

Are you able to answer my daughter's question?

Answer on page 103.

8. MONTHS WITH FIVE SATURDAYS

On the last weekend in July, we invited some of our neighbors over for a small barbecue. The weather was good, and soon the mood was festive in our back yard.

It was almost midnight, when Fred called us together. "What would you think about going bowling together some time?" His idea was seconded with enthusiasm.

"That's a great idea," Helen said, "but we shouldn't just go bowling once—we should do it regularly." The other neighbors thought so too, and we agreed to rent a bowling alley once a month on a Saturday evening.

I offered to reserve the bowling alley, but whenever I called, I was told, "Sorry, we have no bowling alleys available on the weekend." Finally, my last attempt was successful, but not quite as I had wanted.

"On the first Saturday of each month, the bowling club Good Wood reserves all the alleys," the man on the phone said. "On the second Saturday, the employees working for the Smithfield Company bowl here; on the third, the employees of Nortel; and on the fourth Saturday, a church group has it. On the fifth Saturday of the months that have five Saturdays, the bowling alley is available."

"How many months with five Saturdays are there per year?" I asked the man, but he didn't know. I rented the bowling alley nevertheless.

At home, I looked at the current calendar and at some older ones, and realized that the number of the months with five Saturdays varies from year to year.

Do you know how many months a year have five Saturdays—at the very least?

Answer on page 104.

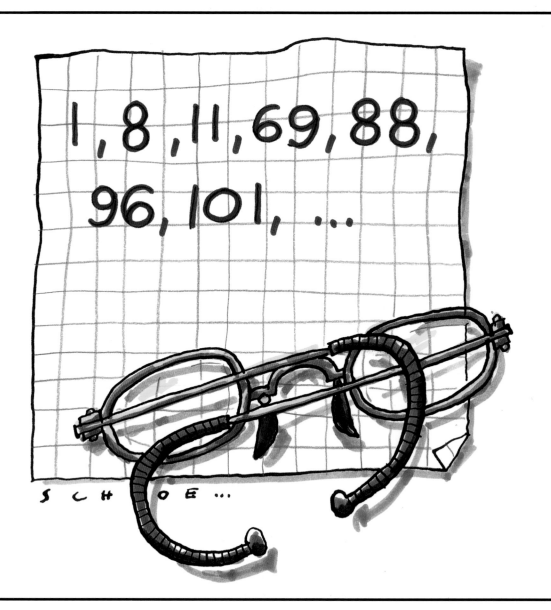

9. THE NUMEROLOGIST

My grandfather always called himself a numerologist. Actually, he was a shoemaker by profession, but his real interest was numbers. He was fascinated by everything about them, no matter whether it was the number mysticism of the Pythagoreans or the abstract theories of modern mathematicians. I once tried to look up in a dictionary what a numerologist actually is, but I could not find the term.

When my grandfather died, I inherited his entire numerological collection. There were dozens of books and several cabinets full of file-organizers that contained his meticulous notes. As I was leafing through the organizers, a single sheet fell out. I picked it up and looked at it. A single row of numbers was written on it, ending in three dots.

1, 8, 11, 69, 88, 96, 101 ...

I assumed the dots meant that you were supposed to continue the row according to the previous pattern. My grandfather had a weakness for strangelings among the numbers, so I wondered what curious common characteristic connected these. It took a while before I was able to continue the row.

Do you know what the next number in this row must be?

Answer on page 104.

10. THE JUMPING GAME

The sun was shining brightly, and I was inside, brooding over my tax return. Outside the window of my office, my daughter Christina and her friend Stella were playing. A little jealous, I watched their game. They had drawn a large chalk triangle and divided it into many triangular fields. Taking turns, they stood outside the edge of the triangle, with their back to it, and threw a pebble over their shoulder. Then they turned and took a big leap into the triangle, hopping from field to field, following rules I was unable to figure out. I knew a number of jumping games from my childhood, but this one was new to me.

I tried to concentrate on my tax return, but did not succeed. After a while, I went outside to join Christina and Stella. "What strange kind of jumping game are you playing?" I asked.

"We came up with it ourselves," Christina answered. "Shall we explain it to you?"

"Yes, please," I said.

"First, without looking, you throw a stone into the triangle," Stella began. "Then you jump onto the field where the stone landed, and hop on one foot into as many fields as possible. You're only allowed to jump into a field that shares an edge with the one you're standing in, and you can only jump into a field one time."

"That doesn't sound too difficult," I said. "Has either of you managed to jump into every field?"

The two of them said no and asked me to try it.

First, I counted the fields within the big triangle—there were 100. Then I threw the pebble and tried to hop on as many fields as possible. I managed 51. On my second try I was more successful and did 58. The third time I cheated a little and threw the pebble onto one of the corner fields, but that didn't help, because I managed only 49. Gradually it dawned on me that it could be impossible to jump on all the fields, and I began to wonder what was the largest number of fields anyone could jump on, according to the girls' rules. But I didn't come up with a result.

Do you know how many fields it could be at the most?

Answer on page 105.

11. THE EGYPTIAN TETRAHEDRONS

August is the hottest month in Egypt; the temperature is almost unbearable—for tourists. The major travel season is spring, but since I was unable to schedule my vacation at any other time, I flew to Egypt in August.

During the first days after my arrival, the heat bothered me terribly, and though my body got used to it eventually, I fled again and again into the pleasant coolness of the museums.

In a small town near Luxor I had gone into a small museum, glad to avoid the midday heat. I strolled through the rooms and looked at the few dusty pieces on display, whose captions were written only in Arabic. Then I discovered a glass case in a corner, housing a number of small stone pyramids. These pyramids were not shaped like the famous ones in the desert near Giza, but they were regular tetrahedrons—shapes created by four identical equilateral triangles. Each of the triangular sides of the pyramids was colored either white, black, or red, which is typical of Egyptian painting.

I asked the museum guard who was standing nearby what purpose these tetrahedrons served, but the man didn't understand English, so to this day I don't know what made the Egyptians build these colorful pyramids. However, the guard had understood what interested me, and unlocked the glass case, so that I could have a closer look at them. I took them out and turned them in my hands. Some pyramids were of one color, some of two colors, and some of three colors. On closer examination, I discovered that no two pyramids had the same color pattern, no matter how I rotated them around.

Do you know, at the most, how many tetrahedrons were standing in the glass case?

Answer on page 105.

12. THE STOLEN WALLET

My brother teaches physics at a high school in Westport. Every week, on Tuesday afternoon, he meets with some students who are especially interested in physics, working with them on subjects that cannot be dealt with in regular class time, setting up experiments and trying them out.

This small physics study group is my brother's hobby. But a few weeks ago, there was an ugly incident, which disappointed him a lot. When the students set up the experiments in the lab, my brother's wallet was stolen. Only a student in the physics study group could have been the thief, since nobody else had entered the room. My brother immediately spoke with each of the five students.

Anthony was indignant: "I did not steal your wallet! Never in my life have I stolen anything. Dana is the thief."

Barbara said somewhat impertinently: "I did not take the wallet. I have a very good one myself. Edward knows who took it."

"I am not the thief. I have not seen Edward today. Dana stole the wallet," Carlos said.

When my brother questioned Dana, she said: "I am innocent. Edward stole the wallet. Anthony is lying when he says that I was the thief."

Finally, my brother spoke with Edward. He said: "I am not the thief. Barbara is the guilty one. Carlos can testify that I could not have stolen the wallet, because I was with him the whole time."

My brother tried to reconcile the five statements, but it was not possible, so he spoke with each student a second time. During that second conversation, all five admitted that they had lied exactly once the first time.

Who was the thief?

Answer on page 106.

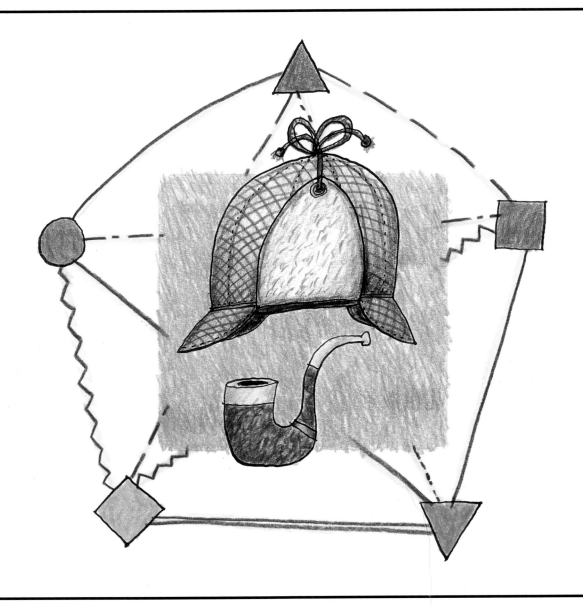

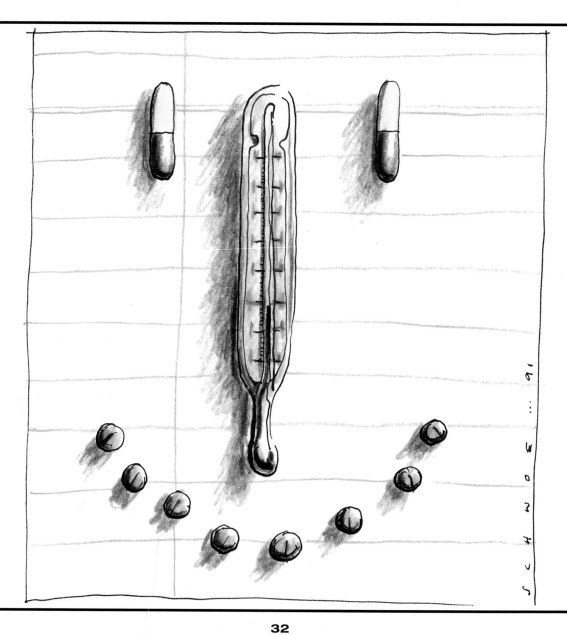

13. THE COUNTRY DOCTOR

Some weeks ago, I had to go to Boston on a business trip. Since I had to take some instruments from my company, I took the car. I was already in Massachusetts, when I heard on the radio that there was a traffic jam on the highway ahead of me. So I left at the next exit, planning to drive to Boston on the back roads.

After some time, I came to a small town whose name seemed familiar. I had almost left town when the reason dawned on me: During my college years I had had a good friend, Charles, with whom I had lost contact. He had studied medicine and taken over a country practice in Massachusetts. I heard somewhere that Charles was living in the village I was driving through. I didn't have to be in Boston until the next morning, so I thought that I would visit my old friend. I found his number in the phone book.

Charles was very pleased about my visit. We had not seen each other for fifteen years and there was a lot to talk about. "Why don't you stay the night? You're not in such a rush and we have a nice guest room where you'll certainly sleep better than in a hotel."

I stayed, and we settled down with a bottle of red wine.

"How is your practice?" I wanted to know.

"I can't complain," said Charles. "I'm the only doctor in a vicinity of 15 miles, and everyone in town is my patient."

"Then I can only hope that these people get sick once in a while," I said.

"I compiled some statistics for last year," Charles said. "The people are actually sick very often: 85% had the flu, 80% had tonsillitis, 75% had circulation trouble, and 70% stomach problems. It does me no harm."

"I believe you!" I looked around the large living room, which was furnished expensively. "If so many of your patients had the flu, tonsillitis, circulation, or stomach problems, then a considerable percentage must have had all four complaints."

"You're right," Charles answered. "I didn't compile any statistics about that, but from the numbers I told you, you can calculate the minimum percentage of my patients who had all four illnesses last year."

I could not. Can you calculate it?

Answer on page 106.

14. THE BOWLING CLUB

Together with a several other couples, my wife and I have been members of a bowling club. A few times a year, we spend a Saturday evening at the bowling alley, and each year in the Fall, we loot our club account and the whole club takes a four-day vacation in Cape Cod.

This year, despite our trip, money was left in the account, and we decided to go with the spirit of the times and buy a computer for the club for word processing and bookkeeping purposes.

Since I am the bookkeeper for our club, I tried to program the new computer along with Erwin, our secretary. Unfortunately, I don't know anything about computers, but Erwin, who is an engineer, is very knowledgeable. It only took him a few minutes to write a small program and then enter the data of the club members into the computer.

"Okay, that's it!" Erwin said. "Now, if you type in the word 'men,' all the names of the couples of our club will come up on the screen. They will all be in order of the men's ages, starting with the youngest." I tried it, and immediately a list appeared. My name was in seventh and Erwin's was in eighth place.

"If you type the word 'women' into the computer," Erwin said, "the same list will appear, but it will be in the order of the wives' ages, starting with the youngest." I typed in the word, and a number of names came up, whereby my name was in eighth and Erwin's in seventh place.

"There is a third possibility. If you type in the word 'couples,' the names will be arranged by the total age of both partners, starting with the youngest." So, I typed in the word 'couples.' This time, my name was in first place, and Erwin's was in last place.

Do you know how many couples are members of our bowling club?

Answer on page 107.

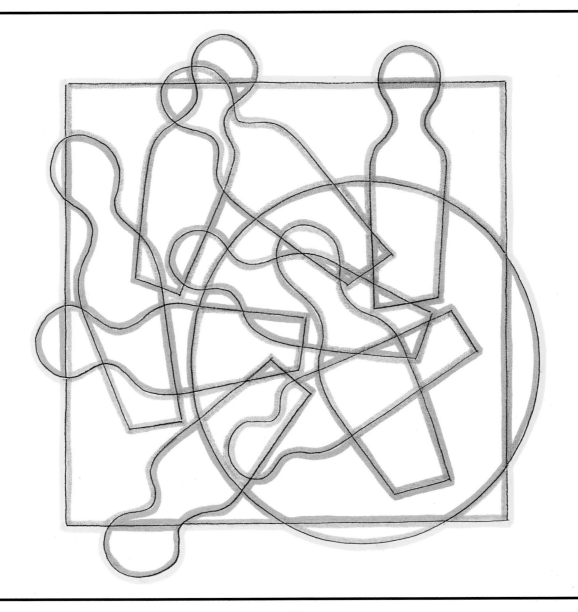

15. THE TWO BUGS

It was a beautiful warm summer day. My wife had gone shopping with the children and I had the entire afternoon to myself. I settled down on a lounge chair in the backyard with a glass of orange juice and a suspense thriller and began to read. Either the book was not so suspenseful after all, or I was very tired, because after a couple of minutes I closed my eyes.

The sun was already low when I woke up. Still somewhat sleepy, I glanced at the empty orange juice glass: Two ladybugs were sitting motionless on it. I sat up to have a closer look. One of them sat on the outer surface facing me, a little bit below the edge of the glass. The other bug had crawled into the glass and sat on the side diametrically opposite to the first bug, a little above the bottom of the glass.

Suddenly, the first bug began crawling towards the edge of the glass. It crawled all the way over the edge into the glass and towards the second bug. After a short time it reached it, and both spread their wings and buzzed out of the glass.

I had been watching the bug closely as it crawled and had been a little surprised about the path it had taken. The thought came to me that the bug might have taken the shortest possible route from its spot to the second bug. This caught my interest. I went into the house and got a tape measure. The glass had a circumference of 12 inches and a height of 8 inches. I remembered where the ladybugs had been sitting and therefore was able to measure their positions as well. The spot of the first bug was 1 inch from the top edge and the spot of the second was 1 inch from the bottom. Now I was able to calculate the shortest path possible for the bug and compare that with its actual path. Indeed, the ladybug had taken the shortest possible route to its partner.

Do you know how long the path of the ladybug was?

Note: You don't have to figure in the thickness of the glass.

Answer on page 107.

16. THE ROW OF CARDS

Once a month on Saturday afternoons I meet some old friends for a game of gin rummy. The card game is only an excuse to spend some time together, and nobody takes the game seriously. Nevertheless, we carry on a certain ritual on these Saturdays: The person who has the most points at exactly six o'clock must make sandwiches for everybody else.

Last Saturday it was my turn. While I made sandwiches in the kitchen with ham and cheese, I heard my three friends doing card tricks in the living room. That happened frequently, when one of us was busy making food, and the tricks were usually pretty familiar.

It wasn't any different this time, until Greg finally said: "Hey! I've got a card puzzle for you!" The other two listened eagerly and tried to solve the problem. Finally, Bob succeeded. "I got it!" he cried, and then he named a playing card. The solution seemed to be the right one.

Then they all started coming up with puzzles using playing cards, and when I came into the living room with my tray, they were so excitedly throwing challenges at each other that they hardly paid any attention to the sandwiches.

"Don't you want to eat?" I asked.

"Right away, but first you have to solve this puzzle," Jim answered. He put 14 cards facedown in a row on the table. Then, he turned over the fourth and the third-to-last card. They were a seven and an eight. He pointed at the eighth card and asked, "Can you tell me what value this card has? All I'm going to tell you is that each triplet of three adjacent cards together adds up to 18."

I am not good at such puzzles, but I tried to solve it, without success.

Do you know the value of the eighth card?

Answer on page 108.

17. FILM FRIENDS

Whenever Tim visits his friend Carl in California, they always go to the movies. So when Carl told him that his car was in the shop and they couldn't see a film, Tim was crestfallen.

"But what about tradition?" Tim asked. "Can't we walk?"

Carl, who wasn't in the best of shape, said, "We could walk, but it's ten miles away. I don't know what's playing, but even if it's won five Oscars, I'm not walking ten miles for a flick!"

Tim had an idea, though. "Well, why don't we bike over? Your roommate has a bicycle, right? He won't mind if I borrow it, I bet."

"I'm sure he'd be happy to let you use his bike," Carl replied. "The problem is that I don't own a bike, so we only have one."

Tim wouldn't give up. He came up with another idea. The two would share a bike. Carl knew that Tim wouldn't take no for an answer, so he agreed to Tim's plan. The two friends started at the same time, Tim with the bike and Carl on foot. Tim biked a distance, put the bike next to a tree and continued on foot. Carl, who on foot was much slower than Tim, after some time arrived at the bike standing by the road. He climbed on and started biking. After some time he overtook Tim. He biked a little further, then he got down, leaned the bike against a tree and continued on foot. After a short period of time, Carl came to the bike and now rode on it for a distance, before he parked it again. Following this pattern, biking and walking alternately, they covered the entire distance from Carl's apartment to the theater and finally arrived at the same time at the theater.

Let's assume that Carl walked at a speed of 4 mph and biked at a speed of 10 mph, and Tim walked at 5 mph and biked at 10 mph. How much time would the friends need to cover the 10 miles?

Answer on page 108.

18. THE GIRL WITH THE BLACK HAIR

I was meeting some friends from my college days in a coffeehouse in our old university town. It was a warm day, and the waiters had set up some tables and chairs on the sidewalk in front of the coffeehouse. We sat outside and drank our coffee in the fresh air.

A lot of people were walking around because of the nice weather. Peter, Warren, and I watched the pedestrians and soon our conversation shifted from mutual memories and acquaintances to commentaries, assumptions, and ironic remarks about the people walking by.

When a pretty girl walked by our table, the three of us followed her with our eyes. "Long, black hair: exactly my taste!" Peter said. "How old do you think she is?"

"I think she's 23 years old," I said.

"No, she's younger," Warren said. "I estimate that she is 22 years old."

Peter shook his head. "I think you're both wrong. She's older than she looks. I bet she's 26."

Unfortunately, we could not find out which of us had guessed correctly, because nobody dared run after the girl and ask her age.

Some weeks later I was invited to a party at a colleague's house. The pretty young girl was among the many guests, and I recognized her immediately by her long black hair. I remembered our estimates and asked my colleague whether he knew how old she was. "Anna's age? Yes, I can tell you that." He told me a number. I was surprised: None of us had guessed correctly. One of us was wrong by a year, one by two years and one by three years.

Do you know how old the girl with the black hair was?

Answer on page 109.

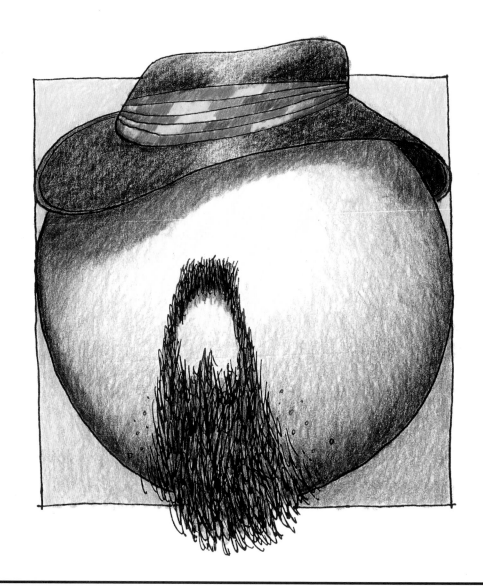

19. THE BALL

When I opened our local town paper on Sunday morning, a headline printed in large letters jumped out at me: "Today—Opening of the Exhibition of the Well-Known Artist Ambrosius Meyer in the Lobby of the Community Center." Since the weather was bad, and we had to postpone a trip due to the weather, I talked my wife into going to the exhibition.

We were the last visitors to squeeze into the community center. Everyone we knew was there. Mr. Barker, a teacher at our school, gave the opening speech, in which he compared Ambrosius Meyer to Picasso. When Mr. Barker finished, the artist himself went to the dais. He totally fit the cliché image of an artist: underneath his wide-brimmed, black hat, which sat crookedly on his head, you could see long hair and a long beard. He wore a frocklike, brightly colored shirt and baggy trousers. His speech seemed rather confused and I didn't understand· a word. Finally he finished speaking, and we could inspect his work.

Evidently, Ambrosius Meyer was enamored of geometric shapes—I felt I was going back to the geometry class of my youth. Everywhere were colorful black, white, striped, checkered and dotted cubes, balls, pyramids, and cones. My wife and I were studying a marble ball, when a voice came from behind us: "This ball symbolizes the unity of shape and number."

We turned around. Ambrosius Meyer stood in front of us. He began a wordy lecture about the artistic statement of his marble ball and finally, looking past us, walked away.

"Did you understand anything?" my wife asked.

"If I understood him correctly, the surface area of the ball in square inches and the volume of the ball in cubic inches are both whole-number multiples of pi," I answered.

"And these multiples are both four-digit numbers," my wife added.

"And then he also said that the radius of the ball is a whole number of inches," I remembered. "But I don't remember what its value is."

Do you know what the radius of the ball was?

Answer on page 109.

20. CELSIUS AND FAHRENHEIT

My little brother Henry had just returned from a trip to Europe. He had been studying in Germany, and now the whole family had come together to welcome him back home and hear about his experiences.

"Is anything really so different over there?" my father wanted to know. "I'm sure life is lived according to completely different rules in India, Kenya, or Japan, but I wouldn't think there was much difference between the U.S. and Germany."

"Of course, if you compare life in those countries, you're right," Henry replied, "but comparing the U.S. to Europe, there are still quite a few differences. For example, I couldn't get used to the fact that the Europeans use the metric system of measurements."

"What do you mean?" my grandmother asked.

"Well, for example, distances are not indicated in miles, but in kilometers; weights are not in pounds, but in kilograms. But most problematic is the temperature. Here in America, we measure degrees in Fahrenheit, while in Europe, they use a Celsius thermometer. In order to convert one to the other, you not only have to multiply with a factor, but you also have to add a number. For example, in order to convert Celsius temperature into Fahrenheit, you have to multiply the Celsius reading by $\frac{9}{5}$ and add 32 degrees. So a temperature of 0 degrees Celsius corresponds to 32 degrees Fahrenheit, and 100 degrees C. is 212 degrees F."

My wife smiled. "That's not such a difficult conversion," she said. "You just take a temperature in Fahrenheit—this one, for example," she wrote a three-digit number on a piece of paper. "Now, you just scratch out the first number and put it at the end, and that's it! You have the temperature in Celsius!

I couldn't believe it and checked the result. It was correct. Nevertheless, I wasn't convinced that this simple method really worked, especially since my wife could not stop grinning broadly. I tried the method with other temperatures. No matter which number I chose, I never got a correct result. Obviously, my wife had taken the only three-digit number with which this unusual conversion method worked.

Do you know which three-digit Fahrenheit temperature my wife wrote on the piece of paper?

Answer on page 110.

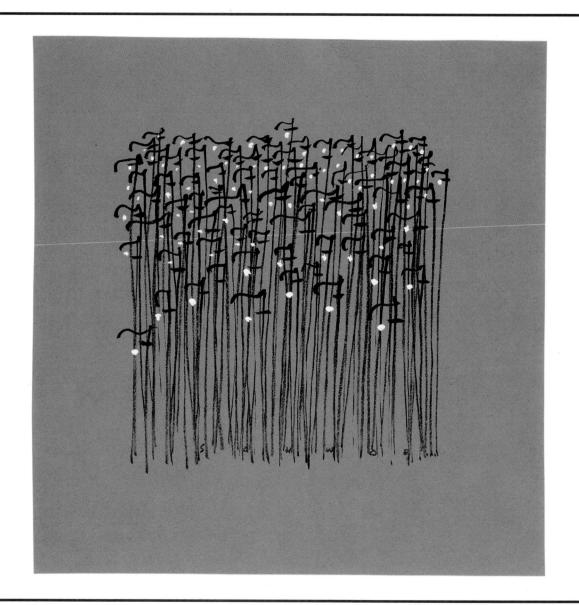

21. THE ARITHMETICIAN

I had gone to Frankfurt on business for a few days with a colleague. In the evening, we strolled through the old town, undecided about what to do. We noticed a sign in the window of a pub:

"This evening the great arithmetician Franz Riese performs! Entrance free!"

"How about it?" asked Ted. "Maybe we should check this out."

I had no objections, so we entered the pub and found an empty corner table. The performance had already started. A man, about fifty years old, was sitting on an elevated platform. That had to be Franz Riese. In a corner, a computer had been set up with a projection screen so that spectators were able to follow the calculations. The guests were asking complicated arithmetical problems, which Riese solved in his head.

"What is 5,111,955 times 20,041,989?" A woman asked.

The arithmetician leaned back, closed his eyes and then said, after about twenty seconds: "The result is 102453745878495." Two young men, obviously assistants of the arithmetician, checked the result with the computer, and everyone could see that it was indeed correct.

The spectators applauded, and then someone asked: "Please calculate seven to the 77th power!"

After a moment, the arithmetician said: "Would you repeat the question please?"

"He's trying to play for time," Ted whispered to me.

The answer came after about half a minute. Riese quoted a very long number.

"He's wrong. His answer is incorrect," Ted said quietly.

A moment later, the two assistants had the answer from the computer. "Unfortunately, Mr. Riese miscalculated," one of them announced.

I was stunned. "Ted—how did you know so quickly that the result was incorrect? Did you calculate that giant number in your head?"

Ted laughed and said: "No, I only determined the last two digits of the number, and those were different from Riese's result. It was quite simple."

I didn't think it was simple at all, because I didn't have the slightest idea how to calculate what the last two digits would be.

Do you know what the last two digits of 7^{77} are?

Answer on page 110.

22. THE VILLAGE MEADOW

The meeting of the village elders was almost over when old Horace Becker, a farmer, wanted to be heard again. "There is one more problem with our new village meadow. Cows, sheep, and goats are all supposed to graze on it at the same time. So I think we should divide it into three individual meadows with additional fences."

An affirmative murmur could be heard in the room. "I believe most of us agree," the mayor said. They voted on Horace Becker's suggestion and it passed.

"In order to avoid trouble from the start, we should make the three pastures the same size," another farmer suggested.

"That is certainly the smartest thing to do," Horace Becker said.

"Since our meadow is square, we can divide it into three rectangular pastures of the same size, right next to each other."

"That won't work," Carol Spencer, one of our schoolteachers, objected. "The small pond that serves as a drinking trough is located in the northeast corner of the meadow. So if we divided the meadow into rectangles, the animals on two of the pastures wouldn't have any water."

They considered all the options, until finally the teacher suggested putting a fence from the northeast corner of the meadow to the west side, and a second one from the northeast-corner to the south side. If it was done right, all three meadows would be of the same size and would have access to the pond. Everyone agreed with this suggestion and decided to hire two workers to put up the fences the following week.

"By the way, how many feet of fence do we need to order?" one farmer asked.

"Oh, well," said the mayor, whose geometry skills were not very good. "How long was the outer fence?"

"1200 feet," was the answer. "Then we simply order 1200 feet of fence again. That will be enough," he suggested.

"And if it is not enough? It would be good if we knew more precisely," Horace Becker said.

Now they all looked at the teacher, who said, after a brief deliberation: "This problem is not so tough. I will order the exact length of fencing we need."

Our village elders agreed with that, and the meeting ended.

Do you know how many feet of fencing the teacher had to order?

Answer on page 111.

23. THE OILMAN'S LEGACY

There was a little olive oil company in our town that was run by an old widower. Even though his three grown sons lived with him, they had other professions and only occasionally did they help their father in the shop.

The old man died some time ago, and he had barely been buried, when the fight about his estate started. His business had not been particularly successful, and except for a few hundred dollars, he left his sons only 21 olive oil barrels.

The three brothers agreed quickly about the distribution of the money, but the barrels led to long and heated battles among the brothers. The problem was that seven barrels were full, seven half-full, and seven empty. Each of the three demanded the seven full barrels for himself and had good reasons for it.

"I am the oldest and I'm the one who worked most in father's shop. Therefore, they are rightfully mine," said Adam.

"To the contrary! Because you were the one who worked the most, you already earned most in the store. I had the least opportunity to work, so I should get the full barrels," argued Ben, the youngest one.

"Since I want to continue running father's store, the seven full barrels naturally should go to me," said David, the middle brother.

And it went on and on, until finally my wife, who happened to be in the shop, made a suggestion: "Why don't you divide the barrels in such a way that everyone gets the same number of barrels and the same amount of olive oil?"

After giving it some thought, the brothers agreed, but they still had reservations.

"Seven full barrels cannot be divided into three equal parts, and the same holds true for the seven half-full and seven empty barrels," Adam said.

"Also, we cannot pour the oil together, since a different sort is in each barrel," Ben added.

"But do all the types of oil have the same value?" my wife wanted to know.

The brothers confirmed that they did.

"Then I can tell you how to divide the oil and the barrels fairly among yourselves, without having to transfer one drop."

"Let's try it," Adam said, and they all went down into the cellar.

My wife distributed the barrels among the brothers, giving only one empty barrel to Ben. When Adam, David, and Ben added it up again afterward, they found out that in fact each of them had been given the same amount of oil and barrels. Family peace was restored.

Do you know how many full oil barrels Adam received?

Answer on page 111.

24. THE GARDEN

My neighbor, Joseph Kimble, rubbed his hands. The old financier Ernest Taft had phoned for an appointment, and that always meant a large order for Kimble's garden center. "This will pay for my vacation," he said to me.

Kimble entered the expensively furnished study in the Taft estate in good spirits. "What can I do for you, Mr. Taft?" he asked.

"Take a seat, Mr. Kimble." The old man pointed to a chair in front of his desk. "I want you to do a major relandscaping of my garden, and I already know how I want it to look." Taft took a drawing from his desk drawer and pushed it towards the landscaper. "You see, there are three trees in my garden—an oak tree, a birch tree, and a lime tree. I planted them at the births of my three children. I want these trees to dominate the garden. So I want you to create three circular lawn areas that will touch on each other, and in whose central points the trees will stand. You can plant flowers and bushes in the rest of the garden."

Kimble scratched his head and stared at the drawing. The three trees were 70, 80, and 100 feet away from each other. He was not exactly good at geometry, and he said pensively: "Well, I'm not sure this will work."

Ernest Taft flared up: "Listen, Mr. Kimble, I'll be paying you a lot of money for your work, and I want my garden to look the way I have it in my mind. It will work!"

Meekly, my neighbor said that he would try. At home, he locked himself in his office and pondered for hours over Taft's drawing, without getting any closer to a solution. He pulled out an old compass from his school days and tried solving the problem with it, but without success. He was about to give up when his apprentice, Max, came into his office.

"You look really upset, Mr. Kimble. What happened?"

My neighbor related his troubles, and Max said, "No problem, sir!" He sat down at the desk, started to calculate and after a couple of minutes gave his boss a piece of paper with three numbers written on it. "There you go! That's the solution!"

Can you also solve Mr. Kimble's problem? What is the diameter of the largest of the three lawn circles?

Answer on page 112.

25. THE WINE CRATE

Friday afternoon I rode my bike into town to buy wine.

"Nice to see you," my wine dealer greeted me. "What can I do for you today?"

Some years ago, I had made a wooden crate for the rack of my bicycle. I use it whenever I buy wine. It is set up so that the bottles fit snugly in the crate and do not rattle, as long as each row and column is full. I gave this crate to the wine dealer and said, "Give me the same wine as usual and please put the bottles in the crate."

The man disappeared into the back room and shortly afterwards came back with the full crate, which he placed on the counter in front of me, groaning.

I paid and was about to go, when he said: "We just got in a new wine—an excellent dry Chardonnay. You must try it. Since you're a regular customer, I'll give you one free." He put the bottle next to my crate.

How was I going to be able to transport the additional bottle? The crate was full, I didn't have a bag on me, and I needed my hands for steering the bike. I must have looked rather at a loss, because the wine dealer asked, "Can I help you?"

When I told him my problem, he said: "The crate is filled with bottles so that you can't move them, but it's not really full. If we arrange the bottles differently, an additional bottle will fit. I'll show you."

He took all bottles out of the crate and started rearranging them. Now he put one bottle less in every second row, but he arranged them so that they were shifted by half a bottle in relation to the previous row. And to my surprise, the extra bottle fit. Now the bottles were not packed immovably in the crate, but the wine dealer stuffed some old newspapers between them, so that they wouldn't rattle while I was riding the bike.

On my trip home, I thought about this problem. I realized I had the smallest possible crate into which an additional bottle could fit.

Do you know how many bottles I had in my crate on my way home?

Answer on page 113.

26. THE TRICK DICE

For many years, I have been meeting two former classmates for a dice game on Wednesday evenings. We always follow the same routine on these evenings—playing the same sequence of games, each of us with our own die. Since throwing dice is a matter of pure luck, we have won equally over the years, and none of us has had major losses or wins.

Two months ago, we ran into Herbert Jamison, who had also been in school with us. We had not seen him for years and invited him to join our game that night.

He seemed to like playing with us, and at the end of the evening, he asked: "Would you mind if I joined you again next time?"

"Of course not," I answered. "We'll be glad to have you back."

During the next months, Herbert joined our circle whenever we played. After some time we noticed that he was winning more often than the three of us. We became suspicious and thought that perhaps Herbert was playing with a trick die. We suspected that it may not have had the usual distribution of dots and maybe the same numbers appeared on several faces. We did not want to confront him until we were sure, so we decided to check his die secretly.

The next evening, during a game, I made up an excuse, left the table for a few minutes, and secretly photographed Herbert's die from behind, while he played.

In the picture you see the three photos that I took. Since you can only see three faces of the die in each photo, they look harmless; nevertheless, from those pictures we knew for sure that Herbert had cheated.

Can you determine what number of dots is on the underside of the die in the first photo—opposite the side with the one?

Answer on page 114.

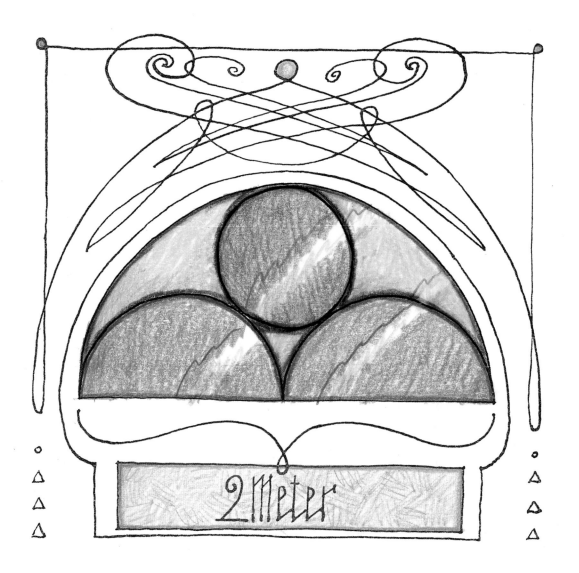

27. THE WINDOW

My wife and I had taken the biggest step of our lives and had bought a house. We had saved for many years to get enough money to realize our dream—with the help of a loan from the bank. We found an art-deco house, built early in the 20th century. We immediately fell in love with it. The house was in good condition, though quite a few things needed repair and modernization. But the price was not too high, so we bought it.

From that day on, I spent all my free time hanging wallpaper, putting down wall-to-wall carpeting, painting ceilings, windows, doors, and laying bathroom and kitchen tiles. After weeks of work, I thought I was finally done.

But when I came home one evening, my wife was standing in the front yard, looking critically at the half-round window above our front door. This window had one circular pane, two semicircular ones, and three in the shape of bow-triangles.

"I just talked to Mrs. Johnson from next door," my wife greeted me. "She says that the panes used to be colorful in the past, and not, like now, just white. Don't you agree that we should restore them to their original look?"

There was no arguing with my wife when she asked such a question, so I agreed and went on my way.

The next day I showed the glazier a drawing of the window. "The circular pane should be red, the two semicircles blue, and the three background areas yellow. Can you tell me how much the six panes will cost?"

The glazier scratched his head and said: "I'll have to calculate that first, because the colors vary in price. The red glass costs $171 per square meter, the blue $160, and the yellow $180. The cutting of the glass is free of charge."

Do you know how much money I had to pay?

Note: You may ignore the thickness of the frame and the borders in your calculations.

Answer on page 115.

28. THE JIGSAW PUZZLE

My in-laws had come to visit and brought a jigsaw puzzle for my four-year-old daughter, Sarah. After we explained that she had to put the pieces together to form a picture, she retreated with the game behind an armchair. We didn't hear anything more from her, except for a low murmuring. After a quarter of an hour my curiosity got the best of me and I peeked over the back of the chair.

Sarah was sitting on the floor, puzzle pieces scattered all around her. She was trying to put the pieces together without any system that I could recognize. She had already succeeded in putting quite a few pieces together in one piece from the middle of the picture. Well, I behave like many other fathers when I watch my kids play: I get restless, I give a lot of advice—mostly undesired—and if it were up to me, I would take everything out of their hands and do it myself. It was the same with the puzzle.

"Why don't you start with putting the edge together?" I asked her. "That's rather easy and after that it's easier to put together the remaining pieces."

In the meantime, my mother-in-law had joined us. "Let Sarah do it the way she wants," she said.

"But when you put puzzles together systematically, it is not so hard. And the best system is to put together the edge first, because these pieces are easier to find, and there are many fewer of them than the pieces on the inside of the puzzle," I, the know-it-all, insisted.

"Nevertheless, you should not force your system on the child," she scolded me. "Besides, it's not true that the edge of the puzzle consists of fewer pieces than the inside. On the contrary, exactly half of all the pieces are in the edge of this puzzle."

I did not believe that, but when I counted, I realized that my mother-in-law was right.

There are only two sizes of puzzle in which exactly half of the pieces form the edge. Sarah's puzzle was the one with the higher number of pieces.

Do you know how many cardboard pieces were in my daughter's puzzle?

Note: Assume that the pieces join together as in a typical jigsaw puzzle and form rows and columns like in the illustration.

Answer on page 116.

29. THE STRAWBERRIES

"Max! Max! Where are you? Come here at once!" My neighbor Joseph Kimble was furious. He ran through the garden center, his face bright red, looking for his apprentice. Finally he found him with Ava, the female apprentice, sitting on a bench behind the hydrangeas.

"What were you thinking?" he snapped furiously. Ava giggled somewhat embarrassed, but nothing could disturb Max's equanimity. "What are you talking about, Mr. Kimble?" he asked.

"I'm talking about the strawberries, of course! You let the strawberries that we picked this morning sit in the bright sun the whole day. Now they are dried out and have become lighter, and I won't get as much money for them." Mr. Kimble looked as if the existence of the garden center depended on these strawberries. But his apprentice did not seem to have a bad conscience.

"Please calm down, Mr. Kimble. Let me have a look at the damage," Max said, and he quickly walked away, before his boss could respond.

Ten minutes later, Max came to Mr. Kimble's office. "It's not so bad," he said. "As you know, fresh strawberries are 99% water. I checked our strawberries. Due to the fact that they were sitting in the sun, their water content shrank to 98%. This one little percent will not ruin you." After saying that, he walked off and left my stupefied neighbor to himself.

How heavy were the dried-out strawberries, if the fresh ones weighed 100 pounds?

Answer on page 116.

30. THE ADVISERS

"Checkmate!" My neighbor Ziggy Dawkins could hardly control the triumph in his voice. Normally, I am the better chess player, but that evening I had lost every game. I must have looked a bit miffed, because Ziggy laughed and said: "You look like King Lorwin."

I didn't understand what he meant.

"Don't you know the Münchhausen story?" Ziggy asked. He leaned back in his armchair and sipped his wine with enjoyment. Then he began to tell the story.

"After Baron Münchhausen left Constantinople, he came to the small kingdom of Frennet. He had been there frequently on his travels, and had always been greeted cheerfully by King Lorwin. But this time, Lorwin made him wait for hours and finally sent a servant to tell him that he had a headache and was going to bed. Baron Münchhausen asked about the reason for Lorwin's low spirits and was told that he had lost a chess game against King Borax, the emperor of a neighboring country.

"King Lorwin was a passionate chess player and he hated nothing more than losing a game. He brought the best chess players in the country to his palace as advisers, and consulted them on every move he made during a game. In the competition against King Borax

they advised him to make a move with one of his bishops that he thought was wrong, but he made it nevertheless. Due to this, he lost the bishop, and from then on the game went downhill, and a short time later King Borax triumphantly cried, 'Checkmate!'

"King Lorwin fumed with rage and chased his advisers into the courtyard, which was paved like a chessboard in 64 black-and-white squares. 'You are all chess bishops now, and you will not leave this courtyard until you have spread yourselves out on the squares in such a way that no one can move to another one's square,' he commanded furiously.

"After Baron Münchhausen heard this, he went into the courtyard and found the advisers at a loss. They were not able to solve the task set them by the king and were fearful of his rage. But Münchhausen was able to help them. He assigned each of them to a chess square. By the way, they were very lucky: If there had been one more person, the problem would have been unsolvable."

"How many advisers did King Lorwin have?" I asked Ziggy.

"I'm trying to find that out myself," he answered, grinning.

Do you know?

Answer on page 117.

31. THE WINNERS

I wanted to see the late night movie and turned on the TV at 11 P.M. My watch must have been a little fast, because the last minutes of the previous program, a game show, were still on.

Obviously the last question had just been answered correctly, because some players were jumping up and down on the stage and hugging each other. The spectators in the hall were clapping enthusiastically, as the camera turned toward the winning team and showed each person in a close-up shot. The master of ceremonies approached the winners and shook their hands. "Congratulations! Great job! You were fabulous!"

After the team calmed down and the applause died down, he said: "Ladies and gentlemen, you have won, but only the last assignment will show how much you have won."

An assistant brought seven large, colorful disks onto the stage and gave them to the team. The numbers 0 to 6 were written on them. The master of ceremonies pointed at a large board and said:

"You have one minute to attach some or all of the disks next to each other onto this board, so that a number with more than one digit results. This number will be the amount—in dollars— that you have won."

He began to smile and lifted his forefinger. "There is, though, a small catch. Since your team consists of twelve players, the number that you create must be divisible by 12 so that you can distribute the sum among yourselves in whole dollar amounts." He paused briefly and then asked: "Have you understood everything?"

The team nodded and took their positions in front of the board.

"All I can do is wish you luck," the master of ceremonies said, and he gave the signal to start.

I began to ponder what number the team had to create so that their winnings would be as high as possible.

Do you know?

Answer on page 117.

32. THE ETHNOLOGIST

I had started my hike through the forest in bright sunlight, but I had not been on the road for long when large black storm clouds approached. They quickly came closer, and the first raindrops started falling. Luckily, there was a hut close by. I had barely reached it when the thunderstorm started, and the rain poured in torrents.

It was rather dark in the hut. When my eyes got used to it, I realized that I was not alone. On a bench at the back wall sat a small old man, who greeted me with a friendly, "Good day, young man. Please have a seat."

We started to talk and it turned out that my companion was a retired professor of ethnology. He told me that even though he was almost eighty years old, he went on a research trip to the Amazon jungle every year.

"Last year I was in a small, completely isolated village near the Rio Negro," he told me. "The special thing about this village was that its inhabitants were either extremely smart or extremely stupid. People with medium intelligence were completely missing. I studied the village people for several weeks and found out that there were more young women than stupid women and more young women than stupid young men."

"What about the children?" I wanted to know.

"Of course I took them into consideration as well. Girls count as young women and boys as young men."

I thought about what he had said for a while, and then I asked, "How many smart people were there overall in the village?"

Somewhat embarrassed, the ethnologist replied: "Unfortunately I don't remember the number. But if you think about it, you can easily figure out how many smart people—at the very least—there are in the village."

I could not.

Do you know how many smart people—at the very least—live in the village?

Answer on page 118.

33. THE ELECTION

Last weekend the new board of directors of our sports club was to be elected. Since I am the secretary of our club, it was my task to prepare for and execute the election. The club is large, so I had to do a lot of work, from finding the candidates and putting together the ticket, to sending it to all the members of the club. I turned the clubhouse into a polling place, and had the hall of the community center decorated for the election party.

All Sunday I sat at the entrance of the clubhouse, distributing ballots and crossing off the names of those who had voted from my member list. At six o'clock in the evening, the counting of the ballots began.

Our bylaws specified that those candidates who together had received more than half the votes could form the board of directors. I favored the brothers Addison, Bruno, and Clement Kendall, who had always been very active in the club, and who, I hoped, would save us from financial ruin. But unfortunately, the three of them didn't make it. Their share of the votes was a little bit below 50%.

As a result, Larry Pullman, the butcher, was able to form a coalition with another candidate and jump the 50% hurdle.

During the post-election party, Larry Pullman gave his victory speech. Unfortunately, he was not a very blessed speaker, and his wordy, boring speech stretched laboriously from minute to minute. It was harder and harder to listen to it, and after half an hour I completely tuned it out.

I started to play around with the numbers of the election results on my pad. I realized that the three Kendall brothers had each received a different share of the votes, and each share could be expressed by a fraction whose numerator was a 1. I added the three fractions together and examined the result. I realized that the sum was the highest possible value below $\frac{1}{2}$ that could be reached by adding three fractions whose numerators were 1.

Clement Kendall received the fewest votes of all three brothers. Can you tell what portion of the votes he received?

Answer on page 119.

34. THE CANOE TRIP

Every summer I go on a canoe trip for a couple of days, all by myself, without my wife and children, in order to relax from my hectic everyday life. I pick a quiet river, pack groceries, a cooker, pots, clothing, utensils, and my tent into the canoe and enjoy a weekend without work, family, and TV. During the day, I paddle on the river, and in the evening I set up my tent in a meadow at the riverbank.

This year I picked a small river that runs about 30 miles north of our town. On the second day of my trip, I took a break in the afternoon near a narrow bridge and cooked lentil soup at the riverbank. After eating it, I drank a glass of root beer and fell asleep in the sun.

It was 3 P.M. when I woke up. I quickly threw my things into the canoe and started to paddle. Since I was going against the current, my progress was slow. I had been paddling along for half an hour, when I noticed a man on the riverbank, who was gesticulating wildly with his arms and yelling something to me. I didn't understand him, so I paddled closer.

"Before—when you had just climbed into your canoe, you lost a bottle of root beer. I saw it from the bridge and I've been trying to get your attention ever since," he said.

"Oh, no!" came out of my mouth. "It's the only beverage I brought with me, and it was almost full." I quickly thanked him, turned around and paddled down the river in order to find it.

I was lucky: two river curves behind the bridge, where I had taken my break, my root beer bottle was drifting leisurely in the water, and I was able to fish it out effortlessly. Then I turned my canoe around again and glanced at my watch: the bottle had been in the river for quite some time. Fortunately I had closed it up well with the cork, and not a drop had escaped into the water.

Do you know how long the bottle had been in the water? The river flowed with a speed of 2 mph, and I had paddled with a constant speed of 5 mph in relation to the water.

Note: You may assume that the conversation and the turning-around manuever did not take any time.

Answer on page 119.

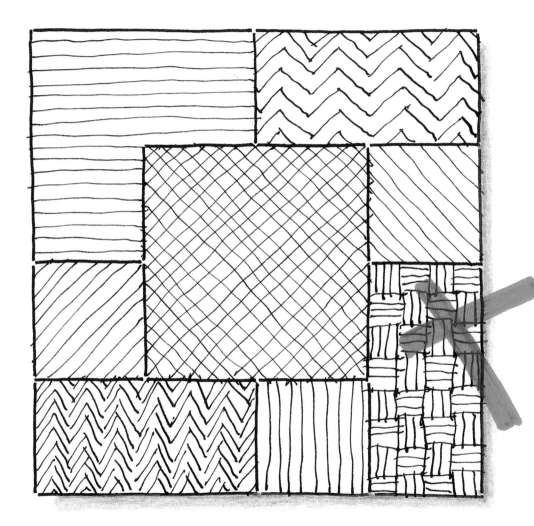

35. THE DOILIES

Aunt Gert is my father's oldest sister. She is single and with increasing age has become a little strange. She spends most of her time stitching or crocheting doilies. Every piece of furniture in her apartment is covered with these doilies; every vase stands on a doily; and there are even doilies on the TV and the washing machine. Everyone in the family receives the products of her untiring hard work: for Christmas, Easter, birthdays, anniversaries, and whenever she visits, we all get Aunt Gert's doilies.

Some weeks ago, it was Aunt Gert's birthday. She was 75 years old, and the entire family went to her place for coffee. We nephews and nieces had pooled our money and bought her a new, larger coffee table. With a lot of effort we wrapped the table with a dozen of sheets of wrapping paper and decorated it with a large red bow.

We carried the table into Aunt Gert's apartment, put it down and sang "Happy Birthday to You." Of course, you could tell right away that what we had wrapped up was a table, but she pretended that she had no idea. "That's a large gift. I wonder what's in it." When she unwrapped the table, she said, "Oh! How beautiful! My old coffee table is much too small. This one is just the right size. Thanks so much, my dears."

Aunt Gert wanted to set up her gift immediately. She cleared off everything that was on her old table, and we exchanged it for the new one. The new table was square, like the old one, but its sides were twice as long.

"It needs doilies," Aunt Gert said. "It's lucky that I have some extra doilies we can use."

Aunt Gert got eight square doilies, all the same size, and placed them on her new coffee table, as shown in the drawing. Then she served coffee and cake.

While drinking the coffee, I wondered about the sequence in which my aunt had placed the doilies on the table.

Can you tell in what number sequence the doily marked with the red cross was put down on the tabletop?

Answer on page 120.

36. THE HAY SUPPLY

It was a hot summer day and I had taken the day off. I went for a walk through the meadows and fields outside our town. I was resting on a bench in the shadow of a huge elm tree when an old man whom I knew by sight approached and said: "May I join you?"

For a long time we silently watched the farmers, as they turned over the hay in the meadows. Finally, the old man said, "If the weather doesn't change, there will be a good harvest this year." I nodded, and after some time he continued, "In the old days I also had a farm. And I remember well the summer of 1946 and the following winter." Lost in thought he stared into the distance and sighed. "I was still young and had misjudged the weather. Just after I mowed my meadows, it rained for days and a large portion of the hay rotted. Well, when it rains it pours. In the fall, lightning struck my hayrick in a thunderstorm and it burned to the ground. I was able to save only a very small part of my hay."

The old farmer began to stuff his pipe slowly and laboriously. Then he continued his story.

"Now the problem was: How could I get my animals through the winter? I had three cows, three sheep, and three goats, and I wondered whether I shouldn't sell some of them. If I sold the goats, the hay would have lasted for 45 days. Without the sheep, it would have lasted for 60 days, and without the cows for 90 days."

"And what did you do?" I asked eagerly.

"Well," the man said, "since I needed hay for at least five months, I would have had to sell most of the animals. I did not want to do that, so I kept them all. During the first months I was not able to buy additional food, so I counted on my luck—and it arrived right in time. I had just fed the last fork of hay to the animals when a neighbor told me that he had sold all his livestock and wanted to move to town to work in a factory. He sold me all the hay he still had for a very low price, and I was able to feed my animals through the winter."

"How long did your original hay actually last?" I wanted to know, but the old farmer could not remember.

Do you know how many days it lasted?

Answer on page 120.

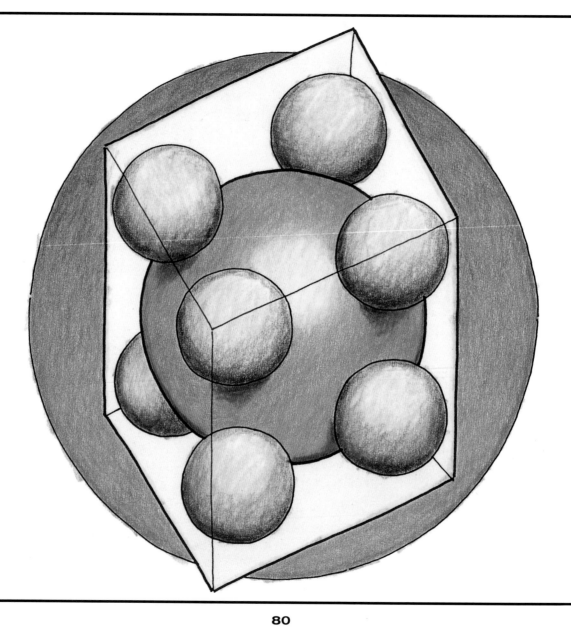

37. THE GIFT

Last Monday was my Aunt Rosa's birthday and I had completely forgotten—it didn't hit me until Friday. I had neither called her nor sent her a card. I went to town with a bad conscience to buy a gift for her, planning to send it belatedly for her birthday.

It isn't easy to find a gift for Aunt Rosa. She already owns everything anyone could wish for, and the windowsills, shelves, cupboards, dressers, and tables in her little house are packed with knickknacks and other trinkets, given to her by numerous nieces and nephews for various occasions. Therefore, my search for a suitable gift was not easy, and I was already totally desperate, when I finally discovered something pretty in a department store. It was a flame-red, thin-walled glass ball, similar to those used as Christmas tree ornaments, only much bigger. The ball had an opening as thick as a thumb at one spot. The saleslady told me that you were supposed to place the ball on a stick and put it in a flower bed in the front yard. She said that that looked very nice.

Back at home, I wondered how I could wrap the ball so that it would arrive at my aunt's in one piece. I found a cube-shaped box with a length of 30 inches, but my glass ball only had a diameter of 28 inches. So that it would not roll around and break in the shipping process, I placed a Styrofoam ball in each of the eight corners of the box. They were all the same size and just big enough so that the glass ball sat tightly in the box. I was able to take the package to the post office without being worried about it.

Do you know the radius of the Styrofoam balls?

Answer on page 121.

38. THE ROW OF NUMBERS

Computers had always been a mystery to me. I had never intended to do anything about that, until I had an experience that changed my opinion profoundly.

My daughter's school was having an open house. Proudly, Christina led me through the building and showed me her classroom. There were several computers in front of which very little children were sitting.

"Are they actually able to use those?" I asked my daughter, astonished.

"Yes, of course, Daddy," she answered. She sat down in front of an unused computer and began to type. Graphics, texts, and symbols appeared and disappeared on the screen. "You see, I know how to do it too."

The next day I bought a used PC and registered for a computer class for beginners at a school for continuing education. I no longer wanted to embarrass myself by knowing less about computers than my children!

A few nights ago I had been sitting in front of the computer the entire evening. "Done!" I sighed contentedly, as my daughter came into the room.

"What's done?" she asked.

"My program is finished." I answered. "Look, the computer asks you to enter two random numbers a_1 and a_2, and after that a third number n, which must be positive and whole. Then the program calculates the row of numbers a_1, a_2, a_3 etc. up to a_n. Starting with a_3, each number in the sequence is the difference between the previous two numbers. For example, $a_7 = a_6 - a_5$. After that, all numbers from a_1 to a_n are added up, and the result is shown on the screen. Why don't you try it!"

Christina sat down and first typed the numbers 5.11 and 19.55 and after that, as a third number, 60,000,000. So the computer had to calculate the first 60,000,000 terms in the sequence, and then add them up. While the computer was working on it, my daughter suddenly said, "I can calculate faster than your PC. I already know the result."

She said a number.

"You're kidding!" I said, but when some seconds later, the number Christina had predicted appeared on the screen, I was quite stunned.

Do you also know the solution?

Answer on page 121.

39. THE DOMINOES

My son seemed to be bored. He went from one room to the next, started a brief conversation with me, then with my wife, and finally fell into an armchair and stared sullenly out the window.

"Why don't you play with your train set?" I suggested. He didn't feel like it. "Then build something with your Legos."

"I don't know what to build," he whined.

I gave up and got wrapped up in my newspaper.

After some time he finally got his game box and took out a bunch of dominoes. He began to build towers, houses, and stairs with the 28 tiles, then arranged them again and again into new rectangles.

Shortly before 3 o'clock my wife said to Matthew: "The Dawkins are coming over for coffee shortly. Would you please pack up the dominoes? I want to set the table."

"Oh, no!" Matthew moaned. "I just made such a great number pattern with the dominoes! I'll never be able to do it again. Couldn't you have coffee at the kitchen table?"

I saw my wife starting to get annoyed. Since I didn't feel like a family fight, I said, "I have a suggestion. I'll draw your domino pattern onto a piece of paper, and after our company leaves, I'll put the dominoes back on the table exactly like they are now."

My son, who probably realized that he wasn't going to win this one, agreed. So I took pencil and paper and drew a frame of 7 × 8 squares on the paper. I wrote the number value of the individual dominoes into the squares. But when I went to reconstruct the domino pattern two hours later, I realized that I had forgotten to mark the edges of the individual dominoes. I tried to figure it out, but I got stuck again and again.

"I can't believe this! It must be possible!" I mumbled.

Matthew, who was looking over my shoulder, asked, "It doesn't work, Daddy? Shall I help you?"

We worked on it together and actually succeeded after many attempts.

Can you reconstruct how the dominoes were placed?

Answer on page 122.

40. THE CHESS TOURNAMENT

The chess club in our town was celebrating its tenth anniversary. For its 22 members, that was reason enough to have a big anniversary bash.

Preparations were in full swing. In the afternoon, ball games had been planned for the children plus sack-jumping and pony rides. A refreshment tent was set up for the adults, and in the evening a cold buffet was planned with dancing afterward. Musicians had already been hired. But the highlight of the anniversary celebration was to take place in the late afternoon—a giant tournament of the club members.

The celebration committee had not yet agreed on how the tournament should proceed.

"I suggest that each member play once against each other member," said my neighbor Ziggy Dawkins, who was the president of the club. "We could set up some game tables in the center of the hall. Then the guests at the festival can watch."

"And who is supposed to get a prize?" Victor Costello wanted to know.

"I've already thought about that," Ziggy Dawkins answered. "In order to make the tournament more exciting, every winner of each individual game shall receive $50. In case of a draw, each player gets $25."

Parker Johnson, the cashier of the club, wrinkled his forehead and began to calculate. "Since we don't know beforehand how many games will be won and how many will end in a draw, it's hard to determine how expensive this tournament will be for the club."

"You are wrong," Ziggy answered. "I can tell you exactly how much money the tournament will cost."

Was Ziggy right? If so, how much money does the cashier have to spend on the tournament?

Answer on page 122.

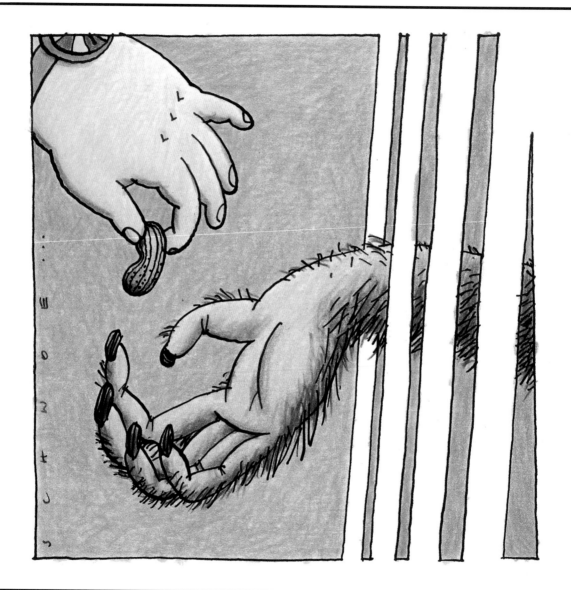

41. THE MONKEYS

My children love animals and we often go the zoo. On Sunday, they were begging me to go again. I gave in, although I would have preferred to spend the afternoon on the lounge chair in the backyard.

"May we feed the monkeys?" Christina asked. I had nothing against it, so they packed a large bag with peanuts and we went on our way.

As soon as we arrived at the zoo, Christina, Matthew, and Sarah started running with the peanut bag. Every time we go to the zoo the three of them run to the monkey house first thing, watch the activities of the monkeys, and feed them peanuts. I slowly trotted after them, looking at the other animals as I passed by. When I arrived at the monkey house after about a quarter of an hour, my children were sitting on a bench with their backs to the cages, lost in thought.

"What's the matter with you?" I asked.

"We want to distribute the nuts fairly among the monkeys, but that's not possible," Sarah said.

"There are 11 chimpanzees in the first cage, 13 baboons in the second, and 17 gibbons in the third," Christina added. "If we give every monkey the same amount of nuts, we'll have some left over. And if we give the same number of nuts only to the chimpanzees and the baboons—or only to the chimpanzees and the gibbons—or only to the baboons and gibbons, each time some nuts will be left over."

"Why don't you just distribute all the nuts in one cage?" I asked.

"That doesn't work either," Matthew said. "If we distribute the nuts equally among the chimpanzees, one nut is left over. If we give them equally to the baboons, eight nuts will be left, and if we give them equally to the gibbons, three will be left."

I briefly thought about that and then said: "I have an idea. You equally distribute as many nuts as possible among the monkeys, and I'll eat the leftovers."

"Agreed, daddy!" Sarah said. "Then you're our fourth type of monkey."

Can you tell the smallest possible number of peanuts my children had in their bag?

Answer on page 123.

42. THE INVENTOR

He was actually a quite unpretentious man and did not look at all as I had pictured an inventor. He led me through his workshops and laboratories and showed me his past inventions.

"Right now I'm working on this device." He stopped in front of a small machine in a gray aluminum case with a number keyboard and many buttons and indicators. "It is a random number generator."

I was not particularly impressed, but this was probably due to the fact that I didn't quite understand what a random number generator could be used for. I asked him about it.

"There are many applications in technique and in research, but I'll give you an example from an entirely different field. You surely remember from watching TV, the old-fashioned machine for drawing lotto numbers. With my random number generator, this could be done much more simply."

He switched the machine on. "With this keyboard I can set a numerical range, for example, from 1 to 1,000,000,000." He typed the two numbers into the device and they appeared on the indicator. "Now, when I push this button, the generator begins to work and produces a completely random whole number between 1 and 1,000,000,000. Why don't you try for yourself?"

I pushed the button and immediately some lights began to blink, but I couldn't hear anything. A moment later, the indicator showed a number that was indeed between 1 and 1,000,000,000.

"If you now push the button a second time, the generator will produce another random number between 1 and 1,000,000,000. The probability that it will be the same as the first one is only 0.0000001%." I pushed the button again, and the generator spat out a second number. It was not the same as the first.

A calculator was lying on the table. I took it and multiplied the two numbers from the random number generator. The result surprised me. "The product of the two numbers is exactly 1,000,000,000," I said to the inventor.

"And strangely enough, none of their digits is a zero, while their product contains nine zeros."

Do you know which two numbers the random number generator spit out?

Answer on page 123.

43. THE LAST WILL

An old man lived in a small house in my neighborhood. Since nobody took care of him, I sometimes shopped for him and carried his groceries up the stairs.

He had been sick for a long time, and some days before he died, he called me over and said, "My whole life I saved all the money that I could spare. After some years I had 100 gold coins, which I hid in a box in the attic of my house. I continued to save, and as soon as I could save another 100 gold coins, I put it into the box in the attic. I soon had another hundred gold coins, and another, and another. Then it became more difficult to save. I was hoping to have a thousand gold coins saved before I died, but unfortunately I have not succeeded."

The old man was exhausted from talking. His breathing was irregular and he closed his eyes. After some time he spoke again in a low voice. "Please do me a last favor. Take all the boxes from the attic. I have only one relative: a grandson who is not yet of age. I want you to visit him on his next birthday and every birthday after that, and give him one gold coin for every year in his age that he is turning on the day you visit him. When you visit him for the last time, all the coins will be gone."

"That's a strange testament," I said, "but I will do what you ask. Let me think about how often I will be visiting your grandson."

I calculated back and forth, but after a while I said, "In order to figure this out, I need to know your grandson's current age."

The old man told me, and I thought a little more about the answer. "Now I know how many times I'll be bringing your grandson money for his birthday. You can count on it that everything will be done according to your wishes."

How many times do I have to bring money to the old man's grandson for his birthday?

Note: You can assume that I did not make any logical or mathematical mistakes in my conversation with the old man and also that I did not overlook anything.

Answer on page 124.

44. DIVISIBILITY PROBABILITY

Some years ago I visited a former classmate, Philip, who had become a math professor at a well-known university. We had not seen each other for many years, and he introduced me to his wife and showed me his new house with many rooms.

His daughter, almost five years old, was sitting in the family room, playing with small, square plastic disks that had a number or a mathematical symbol printed on them.

"Don't you think your daughter is a little young for mathematics?" I asked Philip.

"There is so much to learn in mathematics that it is never too early to begin," he answered. "She already knows her multiplication tables." You could hear in his voice how proud he was. "But we want to see if you haven't forgotten all your knowledge of mathematics."

I winced. During our school years, Philip had continually annoyed his classmates with tricky mathematical problems, and it seemed that he had not changed.

"Look at this number!" he said. His daughter had placed 28 plastic disks in a row, creating a number with 28 digits. "I will now take out some numbers." He removed ten disks from the row: a zero, a one, a two, a three, a four, a five, a six, a seven, an eight, and a nine. The following number with gaps remained:

5_383_8_2_936_5_8_203_9_3_76

"If I now put the ten numbers back into the gaps of this number, in a completely random sequence, how great is the probability that it can be divided by 396?"

I am completely helpless when faced with such tasks without a calculator, and therefore I had to pass when it came to Philip's question.

Can you answer it?

Answer on page 125.

45. THE PROBLEM OF SHAKING HANDS

Times change, and so do customs. When I was a little boy and my parents had visitors, I was always told, "Shake hands with your uncle!" and heaven help me if I refused. Shaking hands was part of saying hello. And today?

On my last birthday, my wife and I invited over three married couples with whom we are friends. One of our guests, a ne'er-do-well philosophy student in his nineteenth semester, only casually lifted his right hand about up to his hip to greet us, he spread his index finger and middle finger to form a V and said, "Hey, man, where's the food?" I don't want to seem old-fashioned, but I do prefer guests who greet me with a friendly handshake and bring flowers for my wife.

The conversation promptly turned to this issue in the course of the evening. I asked each of my guests, and also my wife, how many hands they had shaken at my party. To my surprise, all the answers were different. Of course, no one had shaken his or her spouse's hand and no one had greeted anyone more than once. The opinions about hand-shaking also differed widely. Monica, a former biology teacher, said, for example, that shaking hands was unhygienic, and she only shook hands with people who offered their hands to her—and if there was an opportunity, she would wash her hands afterwards.

Do you know how many guests my wife shook hands with?

Answer on page 126.

Answers

1. THE HEXAGONAL CLOCK

For the hands position of a clock with a blank face always to make sense, the clock must be set up so that at some point in the course of twelve hours, both hands point vertically upwards at the same time. Since the minute-hand and the hour-hand cover each other eleven times in a period of twelve hours (for instance, at 1:05:27), the clock must have eleven sides. Only then can each hand-position point vertically upwards.

2. THE OLD GRAVEL PIT

Mentally turn the square pond of the park by 45 degrees around its center point, without changing the contents. If you now also draw the two diagonals of the pond, the solution will jump out at you: the entire park consists of eight identical triangles, the pond consists of four. Therefore, the pond is half the size of the entire park. Since the park is 4 acres, the pond is 2 acres.

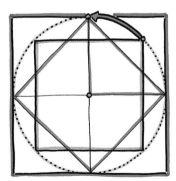

3. THE CHESSBOARD

By placing all the former pieces of the chessboard on top of each other, Matthew was able to saw each piece into two new pieces with one cut of his saw. That means that the number of pieces doubled each time he used his saw. Since $2^6 = 64$, the board fell apart into its 64 individual squares after the sixth cut.

4. THE MATHBOARD

Every number on the board needs to be directly next to, above, or below its next larger and next smaller number. Let's picture the numbers 1 to 60 as pearls strung in rising sequence. The distance between the pearls is just big enough that two adjacent pearls can lie on two adjacent squares on the board. Now it is your task to place the string of pearls onto the board in such a way that a pearl lies on each square. If the pearls 14, 29, and 46 are set at the right spots, you can quickly see that there is only one possible way to place the string on the board. Therefore, the lower right corner square is the number 55.

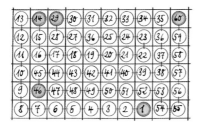

5. THE TABLE

Let's call the dimensions of the cable box a (7 inches) and b (14 inches), and the radius of the table, which was standing in the corner of the basement, touching the walls and the corner of the shaft, r.

From the diagram, we can see that $x_0^2 + y_0^2 = r^2$. Also, $r = x_0 + b$ and $r = y_0 + a$. This means that $x_0 = r - b$ and $y_0 = r - a$. Substituting these two equations into the first formula and solving for r using the quadratic equation yields the following:

$$r = a + b \pm \sqrt{2ab}.$$

Plugging in our values for a and b (7 and 14), we get that $r = 7$ or $r = 35$.

Of course, since the radius of the tabletop must be larger than the length of the cable-shaft, only $r = 35$ makes sense. Therefore, the tabletop had a diameter of 70 inches.

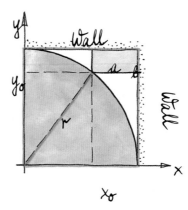

6. THE LOLLIPOPS

If we call the price of a lollipop in the candy store p and the number of the lollipops that Matthew bought there n, then we get the equation $n \times p = 216$. The lollipop price and the total amount are expressed in pennies. For the grocery store, the equation would be $(n + 3)(p - 1) = 216$. If we incorporate the first equation into the second equation, we get $(n + 3)(\frac{216}{n} - 1) = 216$. The relationship now depends on n, the number of lollipops bought. Working out the equation, the result is:

$$n^2 + 3n - 648 = 0$$

This quadratic equation has two solutions—$n = 24$ and $n = -27$. Since a negative lollipop number does not make sense, $n = 24$ must be the correct answer. That means Matthew bought 24 lollipops at 9 cents each at the candy store.

7. THE DIE

Christina's large die had 8 dice in the corners, and 12 dice along the edges. The sum of the dots on the opposite side of a die is always 7. This means that each die along the edge of the large die has 7 dots hidden from view. This means that the sides of the two corner dice that are glued to the die forming the edge also have 7 hidden dots. Since each of the 12 edges has 14 dots hidden from view, 168 dots are invisible.

Therefore, from a total of 420 dots [$20 \times (1 + 2 + 3 + 4 + 5 + 6)$], 252 dots are visible [$420 - 168$].

8. MONTHS WITH FIVE SATURDAYS

Since most years have 365 days and leap years have 366 days, and both kinds of years can begin with a Monday, Tuesday, Wednesday, Thursday, Friday, Saturday or Sunday, 14 different calendars are possible. We must check these fourteen calendars in order to find out the number of months with five Saturdays. The results are listed in the table.

Weekday of January 1st:		Mon	Tue	Wed	Thurs	Fri	Sat	Sun
Number of months with 5 Saturdays	regular year	4	4	4	4	4	5	4
	leap year	4	4	4	4	5	5	4

We see that each year has at least 4, and at the most 5, months with 5 Saturdays.

9. THE NUMEROLOGIST

The sequence that was on the sheet from my grandfather's papers consisted of the first seven numbers that don't change value when they are turned upside down. You can extend it as much as you like:

1, 8, 11, 69, 88, 96, 101, 111, 181, 609, 619, 689, 808, 818, 888, 906, 916, 986, 1001, 1111, 1691, 1881, 1961, 6009, ...

The solution is therefore 111.

10. THE JUMPING GAME

If we color the hundred fields of the triangle like a chessboard, alternately black and white, as in the drawing to the right, we get 55 black and 45 white fields. Since two fields that share an edge are always of a different color, we change the color of our field with every jump. If we start on a black field, the entire tour can consist of 46 black and 45 white fields at the most; there won't be a white field left that we haven't visited. That means we can jump over 91 fields at the most. The line drawn through the triangle shows that it is indeed possible to reach 91 fields.

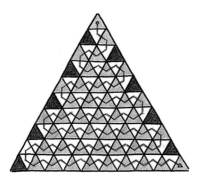

11. THE EGYPTIAN TETRAHEDRONS

There can be only three different one-colored tetrahedrons. In the case of three-color tetrahedrons, each one must have one color that appears twice; that makes for another three tetrahedrons. In the case of two-colored tetrahedrons, the combinations can be white-black, white-red, and black-red. With each of the three color combinations, three different colorations can exist. With the white-black, for example, either one, two, or three sides can be black. So there are nine possible tetrahedrons of two colors. Therefore, in total, 15 tetrahedrons can exist with no two having a matching color pattern.

12. THE STOLEN WALLET

All five suspects had made three statements, one of which was false in each case. If Anthony's third statement was correct, then Dana's first and third statement had to be wrong. But since that it is not possible, Anthony's third statement must be false, and his other two must be correct. In addition to that, Dana's second statement must be false, and the first and third must be correct. Of course, from that we learn that Carlos's third statement was false, and that his other two were correct. From Carlos's second statement, we learn that Edward's third statement is false, and his other two were correct. From Carlos's second statement, we find that Edward's third statement must be false. But that means his second statement was correct, and Barbara must have been the thief.

13. THE COUNTRY DOCTOR

The simplest way is to build up the solution step by step. The minimal overlap of the portion of the patients who had the flu and tonsillitis is:

$$100\% - (100\% - 85\%) - (100\% - 80\%) = 65\%.$$

The minimal overlap between that 65% who had the flu and tonsillitis and the 75% who had circulation problems, is:

$$100\% - (100\% - 65\%) - (100\% - 75\%) = 40\%.$$

In the last step, the patients with stomach problems are added. The smallest overlap of the 70% ill with stomach problems and those who had all the other illnesses is:

$$100\% - (100\% - 40\%) - (100\% - 70\%) = 10\%.$$

Therefore, at least 10% of the patients had all four illnesses last year.

14. THE BOWLING CLUB

Since I was in seventh place on the first list, six men in our club are younger than I am. Their six wives must be older than my wife, in order for the total age of these couples to be larger than my age and that of my wife combined. Therefore, there were at least fourteen names on the second list. On the other hand, there must be one wife who is younger than Erwin's wife, for each man who is older than Erwin, in order for the total age of these couples to be smaller than that of Erwin and his wife combined. But since only six wives are younger than Erwin's wife, there can only be six men who are older than Erwin. Thus, the first list contained fourteen names at the most. Since, of course, the first and the second list were of the same length, our bowling club must consist of exactly fourteen married couples.

15. THE TWO BUGS

In order to solve the problem as simply as possible, we mentally remove the bottom of the glass, cut open the tube that remains, and unwrap it into a flat glass pane. By doing this, we have brought about a rectangle whose one side is the height and whose other side is the circumference of the glass. In addition, we can imagine this rectangle split open flatly, so that we can separate the outer and inner sides of the glass and fold them apart along the upper edge. Now we can recognize the shortest path of the bug: It is a straight line through both spots where the bugs were sitting. The distance x can be calculated with the Pythagorean theorem:

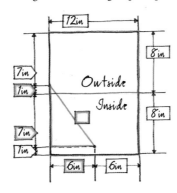

$$x^2 = 8^2 + 6^2 = 100$$

So the bug traveled 10 inches.

16. THE ROW OF CARDS

Since every set of three adjacent cards adds to 18, the fifth and sixth cards must add to 11 (since the fourth card is a 7). This means that the seventh card is also a 7. Since the twelfth card is an 8, the tenth and eleventh cards must add up to 10. So the ninth card must also be an 8. Given that the seventh card is a 7 and the ninth card is an 8, the eighth card must be a 3 to make the seventh, eighth, and ninth cards add up to 18.

17. FILM FRIENDS

Regardless of how the partial sections of the ten miles were subdivided, Kurt had to walk the distance that Carl rode on his bike and vice versa. If we call the entire distance that Kurt walked w, then he biked $10 - w$ miles and spent a total of t hours on the road, where

$$t = \frac{w}{5} + \frac{10 - w}{10}$$

Since Kurt and Carl started at the same time and arrived at the same time, Carl was also t hours on the road. But he rode w miles on his bike and walked $10 - w$ miles, therefore:

$$t = \frac{10 - w}{4} + \frac{w}{10}$$

Since t for both Kurt and Carl is the same, the right sides of the equations above are equal:

$$\frac{w}{5} + \frac{10 - w}{10} = \frac{10 - w}{4} + \frac{w}{10}$$

Solving for w, we get $w = 6$ miles. Therefore, Kurt walked six miles and rode four miles on the bike. Inserting $w = 6$ into either of the first two equations yields $t = 1.6$ hours. So it took Kurt and Carl one hour and 36 minutes to get to the theater.

18. THE GIRL WITH THE BLACK HAIR

Since neither Peter, Warren, nor I had guessed correctly, but also had not been wrong by more than three years, the only possibilities are 24 and 25. But only age 25 also fulfills the condition that one of us was wrong in his estimate by one year, one of us by two years, and one of us by three years. Therefore, the girl was 25 years old.

19. THE BALL

The surface area of the ball is

$$A = 4\pi r^2$$

and the volume is

$$V = \tfrac{4}{3}\pi r^3.$$

These are whole-number, four-digit multiples of π, so the following conditions must be fulfilled for the whole-numbered radius r as well:

$$1000\pi \leq 4\pi r^2 \leq 9999\pi$$
$$1000\pi \leq \tfrac{4}{3}\pi r^3 \leq 9999\pi$$

Those two relations can be simplified to:

$$15 \leq r \leq 50$$
$$9 \leq r \leq 20.$$

Therefore, the radius must be larger than 15 and smaller than 20. Since $\tfrac{4}{3}r^3$ will be a whole number, r must divisible by 3. Therefore, the radius must be 18 inches.

20. CELSIUS AND FAHRENHEIT

Let's call my wife's Fahrenheit temperature $100a + b$, where b is a two-digit number and a is the hundreds place. Her converted Celsius temperature is $10b + a$. Since $F = \frac{9}{5}C + 32$, if $100a + b = \frac{9}{5}(10b + a) + 32$, then her number works. This reduces to:

$$\frac{491a}{5} = 17b + 32.$$

Since a and b are integers, the only number that could work for a is 5. This gives $b = 27$. So the Fahrenheit temperature my wife wrote on the paper was 527 degrees, and that converts to 275 degrees Celsius.

21. THE ARITHMETICIAN

7^{77} means that you multiply 7 by itself seventy-seven times, but in order to determine the last digit, you don't have to multiply everything out.

If you multiply a random number with 7, and you are only interested in the last two digits, you only have to multiply the last two digits by 7. Knowing that, we can find the solution now step by step.

$$7^1 = 7 \times 7^0 = 07$$
$$7^2 = 7 \times 7^1 = 49$$
$$7^3 = 7 \times 7^2 = 43$$
$$7^4 = 7 \times 7^3 = 01$$
$$7^5 = 7 \times 7^4 = 07$$
$$7^6 = 7 \times 7^5 = 49$$
$$7^7 = 7 \times 7^6 = 43$$
$$7^8 = 7 \times 7^7 = 01$$
$$7^9 = 7 \times 7^8 = 07$$

As you can see, the last two digits repeat themselves every four steps. Therefore, if the exponent is divisible by 4, the answer should end in 01. That means that 7^{76} has 01 as its last digit, and 7^{77} consequently ends in 07.

22. THE VILLAGE MEADOW

Since the perimeter of the square meadow, which we'll call U was 1,200 feet, its side, which we'll call a was $\frac{U}{4}$ or 300 feet. Its surface area was $a^2 = 90,000$ square feet. That means that the three pastures each had an area of 30,000 square feet. For the two triangular pastures, we can use the formula for the area of a triangle, $A = \frac{bh}{2}$, where $b =$ the base and $h =$ the height. Both triangles have bases of 300 feet, so their heights are 200 feet. Now, you can calculate the length of the fence with the Pythagorean theorem. We have a right triangle with legs of 200 and 300 feet. We need to buy enough fence for two of these hypotenuses.

$$c = \sqrt{a^2 + b^2} = \sqrt{130,000} = 360.555$$

Therefore, the two fences together had a length of a little more than 721 feet.

23. THE OILMAN'S LEGACY

There are seven full barrels, and seven half-full barrels, for a total of 10.5 barrels of oil. Thus, each son needs to get 3.5 barrels of oil, and 7 total barrels. Since Ben got only one empty barrel, he needed to get 3.5 barrels of oil in the remaining six barrels that he received, without any of them being empty. The only way to do that is to get one full barrel and five half-full barrels. That leaves six full barrels, two half-full barrels, and six empty barrels for the other two sons. Each gets three full barrels, one half-full barrel, and three empty barrels. So Adam got three full barrels.

24. THE GARDEN

If we name the radii of the three circles r_1, r_2, and r_3, and the distances of the sides of the triangles a, b, and c, we can come up with the following equations:

$$a = r_1 + r_2 \qquad b = r_2 + r_3 \qquad c = r_1 + r_3$$

If we now add the third equation to the first, and then substitute in the second and reduce, we get an equation relating to the distances between the trees a, b, and c.

$$r_1 = \frac{(a + c - b)}{2}$$

In the same way, we also get the following equations for r^2 and r^3.

$$r_2 = \frac{(a + b - c)}{2} \qquad r_3 = \frac{(b + c - a)}{2}$$

If we now insert for a, b, and c, the values 70, 80, and 100, respectively, we get the radii 45, 25, and 55. Therefore the largest lawn in the new garden must have a diameter of 110 feet.

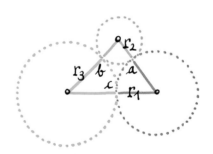

25. THE WINE CRATE

At the start there were n bottles in each row and m bottles in each column. The width of the box is nd, and the height of the box is md, where d is the bottle diameter.

After rearranging, the vertical distance between the centers of the bottles is $\frac{1}{2}\sqrt{3}d$. This is the height of an equilateral triangle whose sides are length d. For an additional row of bottles to fit into the crate, its height would have to be at least

$$m(\tfrac{1}{2}\sqrt{3}d) + d$$

From that, we get:

$$md \geq \tfrac{1}{2}m\sqrt{3}d + d \qquad \text{or} \qquad m \geq \tfrac{2}{2-\sqrt{3}} \approx 7.5.$$

That means, if there were eight rows of bottles in the old arrangement, a ninth bottle would fit into the crate in the new arrangement.

In the old arrangement, the crate contained $8n$ bottles. Since in the new arrangement, in each second row there was one less bottle, now $5n + 4(n-1)$ bottles fit into the crate. The second number must be at least 1 larger than the first number.

$$5n + 4(n-1) \geq 8n + 1$$

$$n \geq 5$$

Therefore, I had 41 bottles in my wine crate on my way home.

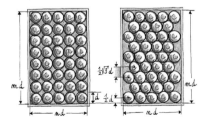

26. THE TRICK DICE

The photos show three views of the die. If we mentally turn the die in the third photo so that the one and the five are in the same position that they are in the second die, the four would be visible on the upper face. But in the second photo, the upper face shows a three. This could happen only if either the one or the five appeared twice. If it were the five, according to the second and the third photo, two faces with a five and one face each with a four and a three would border on the face with the one. But that is not possible, since according to the first photo, one of the four faces bordering on the one has a two. Therefore, not the five, but the one appears twice. The rest is simple. The drawing shows a die flattened out. Therefore, a one is on the underside of the die in the first photo.

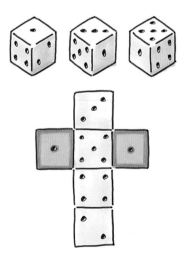

27. THE WINDOW

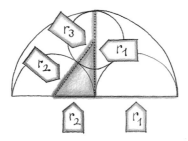

If we call the radii of the window and of the panes r_1, r_2, and r_3, as shown in the drawing, we can calculate the sides of the triangle with the Pythagorean theorem:

$$(r_1 - r_3)^2 + r_2^2 = (r_2 + r_3)^2$$

If we now substitute $\frac{r_1}{2}$ for r_2 and work out the equation of r_3, we get $r_3 = \frac{r_1}{3}$. The area of the circle is calculated using the formula

$$A = \pi r^2$$

so we get the following:

$$A\text{ blue} = \tfrac{1}{4}\,\pi r_1^2 \qquad A\text{ red} = \tfrac{1}{9}\,\pi r_1^2$$

$$A\text{ yellow} = \left(\tfrac{1}{2}\right)\pi r_1^2 - A\text{ blue} - A\text{ red} = \tfrac{5}{36}\,\pi r_1^2$$

If we insert $r_1 = 1$ meter, and multiply the individual areas with their respective prices, then we come up with a total cost of 84π, or $263.89 for the glass.

28. THE JIGSAW PUZZLE

Let's assume that the longer side of the puzzle consisted of a pieces and the shorter one of b pieces. Then, the whole puzzle game is $a \times b$ and the inside has $(a - 2)(b - 2)$ pieces. Thereby, a and b must be at least 3 for the insides of the puzzle to exist at all. Since the inside area consists of half of all the pieces, we have $ab = 2(a - 2)(b - 2)$. If we work out the a part of that equation, we get $a = \frac{4(b-2)}{(b-4)}$. In order to come out with a positive value, the denominator must be positive and thus $b > 5$. If we insert into the equation $b = 5$ or $b = 6$, we would get $a = 12$ or $a = 8$. A b that is larger than 6 will always result in an a that is smaller than b. Therefore, these cases must be ruled out. Only two puzzle sizes are possible, therefore, and they are:

$$5 \times 12 = 60 \text{ and } 6 \times 8 = 48 \text{ pieces.}$$

Thus, Sarah's puzzle consisted of 60 cardboard pieces.

29. THE STRAWBERRIES

In the morning, the 100 pounds of fresh strawberries consisted of 99 pounds of water and one pound of strawberry dry mass. Since only water can evaporate, but not dry mass, in the evening the dried-out strawberries still contained one pound of dry mass. Since the strawberries consisted of 98% water, the remaining 2% had to be this one pound. Thus, since 2% of the weight was one pound, the dried-out strawberries weighed 50 pounds.

30. THE ADVISERS

It is possible to draw fifteen parallel diagonals, which run through the all the squares of a chessboard. If chess bishops are not supposed to be able to move to another occupied square, only one figure can stand on each diagonal. Since the straight lines intersect all the squares of the chessboard, the number of bishops cannot exceed fifteen. But it is also not possible to set up exactly that many, since the two outer diagonals consist of only one square each, and these two squares are on the same diagonal. Therefore, the maximum number of bishops and thus also the number of King Lorwin's advisers is fourteen. The drawing shows a possible set-up.

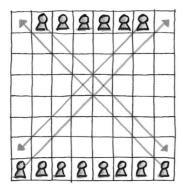

31. THE WINNERS

The highest number that can be formed with the digits 0 to 6 is 6,543,210. But that number is not divisible by 12. Since the sum of the digits in the number is 21, and 21 is divisible by 3, no matter how they are arranged, the number will be divisible by 3. To be divisible by 12, the number must also be divisible by 4 (since 12 = 3 × 4). A number is divisible by 4 if its last two digits are divisible by 4. A little trial and error gives us the best solution: 6,543,120, which means that each player gets $545,260.

32. THE ETHNOLOGIST

The problem here is that it is difficult to visualize the individual statements. Obviously, the village consists of eight groups of people:

1. smart young men
2. stupid young men
3. smart old men
4. stupid old men
5. smart young women
6. stupid young women
7. smart old women
8. stupid old women

With these groups, we can make the following calculation:

all village people	= old village people	+ young men	+ young women	
all stupid people	= stupid old men	+ stupid women	+ stupid young men	
Difference = smart village people =	a	+	b	+ c

The ethnologist does not say anything about old village people, therefore we know only that $a \geq 0$. Since there are more young men than stupid women and more young women than stupid young men, $b \geq 1$ and $c \geq 1$. That means there are at least two smart people living in the village.

33. THE ELECTION

Even though the sum of three different fractions will be smaller than $\frac{1}{2}$ it should be as close to $\frac{1}{2}$ as possible. Let's assume the sum is exactly $\frac{1}{2}$:

$$\frac{1}{a} + \frac{1}{b} + \frac{1}{c} = \frac{1}{2}$$

and that

$$\frac{1}{a} > \frac{1}{b} > \frac{1}{c}.$$

That means that $\frac{1}{a}$ must contribute more than $\frac{1}{6}$, but less than $\frac{1}{2}$ to the total sum. Therefore, $\frac{1}{a}$ can only be either $\frac{1}{3}$, $\frac{1}{4}$, or $\frac{1}{5}$. The fraction $\frac{1}{b}$, therefore, must be larger than $\frac{1}{12}$ and smaller than $\frac{1}{3}$. So the possibilities for $\frac{1}{b}$ are only $\frac{1}{4}$ through $\frac{1}{11}$. And the value of the fraction $\frac{1}{c}$ results from the difference between $\frac{1}{2}$ and $\frac{1}{a} + \frac{1}{b}$.

When you test these possibilities systematically, you come to the solution:

$$\frac{1}{3} + \frac{1}{7} + \frac{1}{43} = \frac{451}{903} = 0.499446 < \frac{1}{2}$$

Therefore, George Kendall received $\frac{1}{43}$ or about 2.3% of the votes.

34. THE CANOE TRIP

If you use the riverbank as your frame of reference, the problem can be solved only by using complicated math. It becomes much easier if you let the frame of reference be the water in the river, in other words, if you consider the water as fixed. The bottle that dropped into the water is not moving in this frame of reference, because it moves at the same pace as the river. The canoe, which had a constant pace relative to the water, was moving half an hour away from the bottle. Because of that, it needed half an hour to get back as well, and that means the bottle was in the water for exactly an hour.

35. THE DOILIES

To solve the problem, it is best to go backwards and remove the doilies from the table one after another from top to bottom. Only one move is possible for removing the top doily. After that, it's not difficult to reconstruct the next steps and to number the entire stack of doilies. The marked doily will be the third from the bottom.

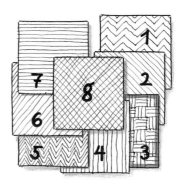

36. THE HAY SUPPLY

If we call the portion of the entire original hay supply that the cows ate in one day C and the portions that the sheep and the goats ate per day S and G, respectively, we can summarize this task in the following equations:

$$C + S = \tfrac{1}{45} \qquad C + G = \tfrac{1}{60} \qquad S + G = \tfrac{1}{90}$$

If we add up the equations, we get:

$$(C + S) + (C + G) + (S + G) = \tfrac{1}{45} + \tfrac{1}{60} + \tfrac{1}{90}$$

or

$$C + S + G = \tfrac{1}{40}$$

That means the farmer's original hay supply lasted 40 days.

37. THE GIFT

Let's call the length of the cube-shaped box A, the radius of the glass ball R, and the radius of the Styrofoam balls r. The center points of the eight Styrofoam balls stuck in the corners of the box form the corners of a cube with length $a = A - 2r$. The diagonal length of this smaller cube is $a\sqrt{3}$, and is also $2r + 2R$. Therefore, $a\sqrt{3} = 2r + 2R$. If we substitute $A - 2r$ for a, we get, after several transformations:

$$r = \frac{(A\sqrt{3} - 2R)}{2(1 + \sqrt{3})}$$

With $A = 30$ and $R = 14$, the radius of the Styrofoam balls is $r = 4.385$ inches.

38. THE ROW OF NUMBERS

The two first numbers of the sequence with sixty million elements are a_1 and a_2, and all other numbers are calculated with the equation $a_i = a_{i-1} - a_{i-2}$. Six consecutive numbers in the sequence therefore are:

$$a_i = a_{i-1} - a_{i-2}$$
$$a_{i+1} = a_i - a_{i-1} = (a_{i-1} - a_{i-2}) - a_{i-1} = -a_{i-2}$$
$$a_{i+2} = a_{i+1} - a_i = -a_{i-2} - (a_{i-1} - a_{i-2}) = -a_{i-1}$$
$$a_{i+3} = a_{i+2} - a_i = -a_{i-1} - (-a_{i-2}) = -a_{i-1} + a_{i-2}$$
$$a_{i+4} = a_{i+3} - a_{i+2} = (-a_{i-1} + a_{i-2}) + a_{i-1} = a_{i-2}$$
$$a_{i+5} = a_{i+4} - a_{i+3} = a_{i-2} - (-a_{i-1} + a_{i-2}) = a_{i-1}$$

Their sum is 0. Since any set of six consecutive numbers will add up to 0, and since 60,000,000 consists of 10,000,000 groups of 6 consecutive numbers, the total of all the elements is 0. The values of a_1 and a_2 do not matter. Therefore, the solution we are looking for is 0.

39. THE DOMINOES

Most of the 28 dominoes can lie in many positions in the pattern at the beginning, but there is only one possibility for the tiles (0-0), (2-2), (5-5) and (6-6). When you have placed these tiles in the rectangle, you'll see that tile (5-6) must go in the second row from the bottom and the tile (4-4) must be in the lower right corner. This means the (4-2) tile has to be in the top row. Continuing this way, there is only one possible solution, as shown.

5	1	0	4	2	1	6	1
3	1	0	4	3	2	0	3
5	2	3	1	3	3	4	0
4	5	3	5	0	6	0	5
2	2	6	2	4	1	6	3
0	6	4	5	6	1	5	4
1	2	6	6	2	0	5	4

40. THE CHESS TOURNAMENT

Since all the members played against each other once, and the club had 22 members, each member had to play exactly 21 games. Since in each game two members played each other, $\frac{1}{2} \times 22 \times 21 = 231$ games took place. Every game cost $50, which would be taken out of the club account and given either to the winner, or in a game that ended in a draw, half to each player. Therefore, the cashier of the chess club had to spend $231 \times \$50 = \$11,550$ for prizes in the tournament.

41. THE MONKEYS

Let's say that N is the total number of peanuts. If N peanuts are distributed among the 11 chimpanzees, every monkey would get n nuts, and one nut would remain. But if N were distributed among the 13 baboons, every animal would receive m nuts, and 8 nuts would remain. Therefore, $N = 11n + 1 = 13m + 8$. This works out to $11n - 13m = 7$. The smallest numbers that fulfill these conditions, are $n = 3$ and $m = 2$, and therefore $N = 34$. Since $11 \times 13 = 143$, every number $N = 143k + 34$ (where k is an integer) results in remainders of 1 when divided by 11 and 8 when divided by 13. Now, all we have to do is to check the numbers to see if they result in a remainder of 3 when divided by the number of gibbons (17), and make sure they're not divisible by the total of any two types of apes, those numbers being $11 + 17 = 28$, $13 + 17 = 30$, and $11 + 13 + 41$. The smallest number to fulfill all these conditions is $143 \times 15 + 34 = 2179$. That means the children had 2,179 nuts in their bag.

42. THE INVENTOR

You can make every positive whole number into a product of prime numbers. For very large numbers, these prime factors are not always easy to find, but for 1,000,000,000, it is no problem: $1,000,000,000 = 10^9 = (2 \times 5)^9 = 2^9 \times 5^9$. Therefore, the prime factors of 1,000,000,000 are only twos and fives.

In order to find the looked-for numbers m and n, which do not contain any zeros and whose product results in 1,000,000,000, you must divide these eighteen prime numbers into two groups. If one group contains both twos and fives, the product definitely ends with a zero, because $2 \times 5 = 10$. So if m and n are not to end in zeros, the twos and the fives must remain strictly separate. Consequently, there is only one possible pair of candidates for the solution: $m = 2^9$ and $n = 5^9$. If you multiply these exponential numbers, you realize that indeed they do not have any zeros, so they are the solution we have been looking for. Therefore, the random number generator spit out the numbers 512 and 1,953,125.

43. THE LAST WILL

Let's say a represents the age of the grandson, and b stands for the birthday visits. Since the grandson was not yet of age, a must be smaller than 18: $0 \leq a < 18$. According to the grandfather's wish, I was supposed to give the grandson as many coins as the years of his age for each birthday, until the entire inheritance was used up. Thus, the paid-out amounts form an arithmetic row:

$$(a + 1) + (a + 2) + (a + 3) + \ldots + (a + b) = ab + \tfrac{b}{2}(b + 1)$$

Since the old man had saved at least 400, but at most 900 coins, this sum must be between 400 and 900, and it must be a whole-number multiple of 100.

$$ab + \tfrac{b}{2}(b + 1) = 100n \text{ with } n = 4, 5, 6, 7, 8, 9$$

From this equation, you easily get six whole-numbered solutions:

b:	25	25	25	25	35	40
a:	3	7	11	15	2	2
n:	4	5	6	7	7	9

Since, when I was told the grandson's age, I knew how often I had to visit him, it can't be that the grandson is 2, because then I wouldn't know if I were to visit him 35 times or 40. So a can't be 2. Therefore, I have to bring money to the old man's grandson for 25 years.

44. DIVISIBILITY PROBABILITY

In order to solve this problem without trying out the 10! = 3,628,800 possibilities, you need to know some divisibility rules:

A number is divisible by 4 without any remainder when the number formed by its last two digits is divisible by 4. The first digits do not matter. For example, 3,141,592 is divisible by 4, because 92 can be divided by 4.

A number is divisible by 9 when the sum of its digits is divisible by 9. For example, the sum of the digits in the number 5,111,955 is 27. Since 27 can be divided by 9, the number 5,111,955 also must be divisible by 9.

The divisibility rule for the 11 is somewhat more complicated. First, you need to calculate the eleven remainder—the difference between two total numbers of digits: the sum of the numbers in the odd positions (those in the first, third, fifth positions, etc.) and the sum of the numbers in the even positions.

For example, the eleven-remainder of 487,259 has the value 3, because 8 + 2 + 9 = 19 and 4 + 7 + 5 = 16. When we subtract one from the other, we get 19 − 16 = 3, so the number is not divisible by 11.

If the eleven-remainder of a number is divisible by 11, then the number itself is too.

Now about the actual solution of the problem. The number:

$$N = 5\_383\_8\_2\_936\_5\_8\_203\_9\_3\_76$$

ends in 76. Since 76 is divisible by 4, N must be also.

The total number of the digits in the number, including those that still have to be inserted from 0 to 9, is 135. This number is divisible by 9; consequently, N can also be divided by 9.

No numbers have to be inserted in the even positions of N. Therefore, the total number of even digits is 73. The ten numbers that still have to be inserted all belong to the uneven positions. Therefore, the total number of digits in the odd positions is easy to calculate. The eleven-remainder therefore results in 73 − 62 = 11. The number 11, of course, is divisible by 11, consequently, N is as well.

Thus, the number N is, independent of how the ten numbers are inserted, always divisible by 4, 9, and 11. N is also always divisible by their product $4 \times 9 \times 11 = 396$. Therefore, the probability of the number being divisible by 396 is 1 or 100%.

45. THE PROBLEM OF SHAKING HANDS

At first glance, it looks as if the problem is unsolvable: information seems to be missing. But that is wrong. The question can be answered without additional information. To do that, let's depict the eight participants in my birthday party with dots that are arranged in a circle.

Since the eight persons didn't shake hands with their married partners or with themselves, each person could shake six hands at the most. But when I asked, the answers that I got, were 0, 1, 2, 3, 5, and 6.

Since no specific names are connected with the letters A to H, we can randomly assume that A shook hands with six people—that is with B, C, D, E, F and G. This is indicated by the lines connecting the squares.

Now we can see in the diagram that it is H who did not shake hands with anybody. Since A shook hands with everybody except with H, we can assume that A and H are married to each other.

In the next step, we will assume that B shook hands with five people. We can see from the diagram that G shook hands only with A, and that B shook hands with everybody except G and H. Since H is married to A, G and B also must be a married couple.

The third step is along the same lines. We assume that C shook hands with four people and then realize that F shook hands with only two people and is married to C.

Now, when we look at the drawing, we can see that D and E each greeted three guests with a handshake. But since I only once received the answer "3" to my question, I myself must be one of the two. Since, in addition, D and E are married to each other, my wife is the second one. Therefore, my wife shook hands with three guests.

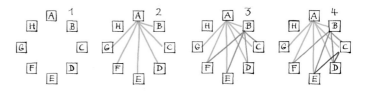

ABOUT THE AUTHOR

Born in Northern Germany in 1955, Heinrich Hemme studied physics and has worked as a physicist for the Philipps Laboratories since 1988. In 1993 he received a chair in physics at one of Germany's most famous institutions for technical studies. While physics is his profession, mathematical puzzles are his passion. Since 1984 he has written over 400 articles and eight books of mathematical puzzles.

INDEX